ONCE THERE WAS A WAR

Born in Salinas, California, in 1902, John Steinbeck grew up in a fertile agricultural valley about twenty-five miles from the Pacific Coast—and both valley and coast would serve as settings for some of his best fiction. In 1919 he went to Stanford University, where he intermittently enrolled in literature and writing courses until he left in 1925 without taking a degree. During the next five years he supported himself as a laborer and journalist in New York City, all the time working on his first novel, *Cup of Gold* (1929). After marriage and a move to Pacific Grove, he published two California fictions, *The Pastures of Heaven* (1932) and *To a God Unknown* (1933), and worked on short stories later collected in *The Long Valley* (1938). Popular success and financial security came only with *Tortilla Flat* (1935), stories about Monterey's paisanos. A ceaseless experimenter throughout his career, Steinbeck changed courses regularly. Three powerful novels of the late 1930s focused on the California laboring class: *In Dubious Battle* (1936), *Of Mice and Men* (1937), and the book considered by many his finest, *The Grapes of Wrath* (1939). Early in the 1940s, Steinbeck became a filmmaker with *The Forgotten Village* (1941) and a serious student of marine biology with *Sea of Cortez* (1941). He devoted his services to the war, writing *Bombs Away* (1942) and the controversial play-novelette *The Moon Is Down* (1942). *Cannery Row* (1945), *The Wayward Bus* (1947), *The Pearl* (1947), *A Russian Journal* (1948), another experimental drama, *Burning Bright* (1950), and *The Log from The Sea of Cortez* (1951) preceded publication of the monumental *East of Eden* (1952), an ambitious saga of the Salinas Valley and his own family's history. The last decades of his life were spent in New York City and Sag Harbor with his third wife, with whom he traveled widely. Later books include *Sweet Thursday* (1954), *The Short Reign of Pippin IV: A Fabrication* (1957), *Once There Was a War* (1958), *The Winter of Our Discontent* (1961), *Travels with Charley in Search of America* (1962), *America and Americans* (1966), and the posthumously published *Journal of a Novel: The* East of Eden *Letters* (1969), *Viva Zapata!* (1975), *The Acts of King Arthur and His Noble Knights* (1976), and *Working Days: The Journals of* The Grapes of Wrath (1989). He died in 1968, having won a Nobel Prize in 1962.

JOHN STEINBECK

Once There Was a War

PENGUIN BOOKS

PENGUIN BOOKS
Published by the Penguin Group
Penguin Books USA Inc., 375 Hudson Street,
New York, New York 10014, U.S.A.
Penguin Books Ltd, 27 Wrights Lane, London W8 5TZ, England
Penguin Books Australia Ltd, Ringwood, Victoria, Australia
Penguin Books Canada Ltd, 10 Alcorn Avenue,
Toronto, Ontario, Canada M4V 3B2
Penguin Books (N.Z.) Ltd, 182–190 Wairau Road,
Auckland 10, New Zealand

Penguin Books Ltd, Registered Offices:
Harmondsworth, Middlesex, England

First published in the United States of America by
The Viking Press, Inc., 1958
First published in Penguin Books 1977
Reissued in Penguin Books 1986
This edition published in Penguin Books 1994

10 9 8 7 6 5 4 3 2 1

The dispatches in this book appeared in the *New York Herald Tribune*
and other newspapers.

LIBRARY OF CONGRESS CATALOGING IN PUBLICATION DATA
Steinbeck, John, 1902–1968.
Once there was a war.
1. World War, 1939–1945—Addresses, essays, lectures.
I. Title.
D743.S65 1986   940.53   86–2392
ISBN 0 14 01.8747 2

Printed in the United States of America
Set in Granjon

Introduction

*   *

ONCE THERE WAS A WAR:
AN INTRODUCTION

ONCE UPON A TIME there was a war, but so long
ago and so shouldered out of the way by other wars and other
kinds of wars that even people who were there are apt to
forget. This war that I speak of came after the plate armor
and longbows of Crécy and Agincourt and just before the
little spitting experimental atom bombs of Hiroshima and
Nagasaki.

I attended a part of that war, you might say visited it,
since I went in the costume of a war correspondent and
certainly did not fight, and it is interesting to me that I do
not remember very much about it. Reading these old reports
sent in with excitement at the time brings back images and
emotions completely lost.

Perhaps it is right or even necessary to forget accidents,
and wars are surely accidents to which our species seems
prone. If we could learn from our accidents it might be well

to keep the memories alive, but we do not learn. In ancient Greece it was said that there had to be a war at least every twenty years because every generation of men had to know what it was like. With us, we must forget, or we could never indulge in the murderous nonsense again.

The war I speak of, however, may be memorable because it was the last of its kind. Our Civil War has been called the last of the "gentlemen's wars," and the so-called Second World War was surely the last of the long global wars. The next war, if we are so stupid as to let it happen, will be the last of any kind. There will be no one left to remember anything. And if that is how stupid we are, we do not, in a biologic sense, deserve survival. Many other species have disappeared from the earth through errors in mutational judgment. There is no reason to suppose that we are immune from the immutable law of nature which says that over-armament, over-ornamentation, and, in most cases, over-integration are symptoms of coming extinction. Mark Twain in *A Connecticut Yankee* uses the horrifying and possible paradox of the victor's being killed by the weight of the vanquished dead.

But all this is conjecture, no matter how possible it may be. The strange thing is that my dim-remembered war has become as hazy as conjecture. My friend Jack Wagner was in the First World War. His brother Max was in the Second World War. Jack, in possessive defense of the war he knew, always referred to it as the Big War, to his brother's disgust. And of course the Big War is the war you knew.

But do you know it, do you remember it, the drives, the attitudes, the terrors, and, yes, the joys? I wonder how many men who were there remember very much.

I have not seen these accounts and stories since they were

written in haste and telephoned across the sea to appear as immediacies in the *New York Herald Tribune* and a great many other papers. That was the day of the Book by the War Correspondent, but I resisted that impulse, believing or saying I believed that unless the stories had validity twenty years in the future they should stay on the yellowing pages of dead newspaper files. That I have got them out now is not for my first reason given at all. Reading them over after all these years, I realize not only how much I have forgotten but that they are period pieces, the attitudes archaic, the impulses romantic, and, in the light of everything that has happened since, perhaps the whole body of work untrue and warped and one-sided.

The events set down here did happen. But on rereading this reportage, my memory becomes alive to the other things, which also did happen and were not reported. That they were not reported was partly a matter of orders, partly traditional, and largely because there was a huge and gassy thing called the War Effort. Anything which interfered with or ran counter to the War Effort was automatically bad. To a large extent judgment about this was in the hands of the correspondent himself, but if he forgot himself and broke any of the rules, there were the Censors, the Military Command, the Newspapers, and finally, most strong of all in discipline, there were the war-minded civilians, the Noncombatant Commandos of the Stork Club, of *Time* Magazine and *The New Yorker,* to jerk a correspondent into line or suggest that he be removed from the area as a danger to the War Effort. There were citizens' groups helping with tactics and logistics; there were organizations of mothers to oversee morals, and by morals I mean not only sexual morals but also such things as gambling and helling around in general. Secrecy was a whole field in itself. Perhaps our whole miasmic hysteria about secrecy for the last twenty years had its birth during this period. Our obsession with secrecy had a perfectly legitimate beginning in a fear that knowledge of troop-ship sailings would and often did attract the wolf packs of submarines. But from there it got out of hand until finally facts available in any library in the world came to be carefully guarded secrets, and the most carefully guarded secrets were known by everyone.

I do not mean to indicate that the correspondent was harried and pushed into these rules of conduct. Most often he carried his rule book in his head and even invented restrictions for himself in the interest of the War Effort. When The Viking Press decided to print these reports in book form, it was suggested that, now that all restrictions were off, I should take out the "Somewhere in So-and-So" dateline and put in the places where the events occurred. This is impossible. I was so secret that I don't remember where they happened.

The rules, some imposed and some self-imposed, are amusing twenty years later. I shall try to remember a few of them. There were no cowards in the American Army, and of all the brave men the private in the infantry was the bravest and noblest. The reason for this in terms of the War Effort is obvious. The infantry private had the dirtiest, weariest, least rewarding job in the whole war. In addition to being dangerous and dirty, a great many of the things he had to do were stupid. He must therefore be reassured that these things he knew to be stupid were actually necessary and wise, and that he was a hero for doing them. Of course no one even casually inspected the fact that the infantry private had no choice.

If he exercised a choice, he was either executed immediately or sent to prison for life.

A second convention was that we had no cruel or ambitious or ignorant commanders. If the disorganized insanity we were a part of came a cropper, it was not only foreseen but a part of a grander strategy out of which victory would emerge.

A third sternly held rule was that five million perfectly normal, young, energetic, and concupiscent men and boys had for the period of the War Effort put aside their habitual preoccupation with girls. The fact that they carried pictures of nude girls, called pin-ups, did not occur to anyone as a paradox. The convention was the law. When Army Supply ordered X millions of rubber contraceptive and disease-preventing items, it had to be explained that they were used to keep moisture out of machine-gun barrels—and perhaps they did.

Since our Army and Navy, like all armies and navies, were composed of the good, the bad, the beautiful, the ugly, the cruel, the gentle, the brutal, the kindly, the strong, and the weak, this convention of general nobility might seem to have been a little hard to maintain, but it was not. We were all a part of the War Effort. We went along with it, and not only that, we abetted it. Gradually it became a part of all of us that the truth about anything was automatically secret and that to trifle with it was to interfere with the War Effort. By this I don't mean that the correspondents were liars. They were not. In the pieces in this book everything set down happened. It is in the things not mentioned that the untruth lies.

When General Patton slapped a sick soldier in a hospital and when our Navy at Gela shot down fifty-nine of our own troop carriers, General Eisenhower personally asked the war correspondents not to send the stories because they would be bad for morale at home. And the correspondents did not file the stories. Of course the War Department leaked to a local newsman and the stories got printed anyway, but no one in the field contributed to that bit of treason to the War Effort.

Meanwhile strange conventional stories were born and duly reported. One of the oddest concerned the colonel or general in the Air Force whose duty required that he stay in reluctant comfort on the ground and who ate his heart out to be with his "boys" out on mission over Germany among the red flak. It was hard, stern duty that kept him grounded, and much harder than flying missions. I don't know where this one started, but it doesn't sound as though it came from enlisted personnel. I never met a bomber crew which wouldn't have taken on this sterner duty at the drop of a hat. They may have been a little wild, but they weren't that crazy.

Reading over these old reports, I see that again and again sentences were removed by censor. I have no idea what it was that was removed. Correspondents had no quarrel with censors. They had a tough job. They didn't know what might be brought up against them. No one could discipline them for eliminating, and so in self-preservation they eliminated pretty deeply. Navy censors were particularly sensitive to names of places, whether they had any military importance or not. It was the safest way. Once when I felt a little bruised by censorship I sent through Herodotus's account of the battle of Salamis fought between the Greeks and Persians in 480 B.C., and since there were place names involved, albeit classical ones, the Navy censors killed the whole story.

We really tried to observe the censorship rules, even knowing that a lot of them were nonsense, but it was very hard to know what the rules were. They had a way of changing with the commanding officer. Just when you thought you knew what you could send, the command changed and you couldn't send that at all.

The correspondents were a curious, crazy, and yet responsible crew. Armies by their nature, size, complication, and command are bound to make mistakes, mistakes which can be explained or transmuted in official reports. It follows that military commanders are a little nervous about reporters. They are restive about people breathing down their necks, particularly experts. And it was true that many of the professional war correspondents had seen more wars and more kinds of wars than anybody in the Army or Navy. Capa, for example, had been through the Spanish War, the Ethiopian War, the Pacific War. Clark Lee had been at Corregidor and before that in Japan. If the regular Army and Navy didn't much like the war correspondents, there was nothing they could do about it, because these men were the liaison with the public. Furthermore many of them had become very well known and had enormous followings. They were syndicated from one end of the nation to the other. Many of them had established their methods and their styles. A few had become prima donnas, but not many. Ernie Pyle was so popular and so depended on by readers at home that in importance he much outranked most general officers.

To this hard-bitten bunch of professionals I arrived as a Johnny-come-lately, a sacred cow, a kind of tourist. I think they felt that I was muscling in on their hard-gained territory. When, however, they found that I was not duplicating their work, was not reporting straight news, they were very kind to me and went out of their way to help me and to instruct me in the things I didn't know. For example, it was Capa who gave me the best combat advice I ever heard. It was, "Stay where you are. If they haven't hit you, they haven't seen you." And then Capa had to go and step on a land mine in Viet-Nam, just when he was about to retire from the whole terrible, futile business. And Ernie Pyle got it between the eyes from a sniper on the trip he planned as his weary last.

All of us developed our coy little tricks with copy. Reading these old pieces, I recognize one of mine. I never admitted having seen anything myself. In describing a scene I invariably put it in the mouth of someone else. I forget why I did this. Perhaps I felt that it would be more believable if told by someone else. Or it is possible that I felt an interloper, an eavesdropper on the war, and was a little bit ashamed of being there at all. Maybe I was ashamed that I could go home and soldiers couldn't. But it was often neither safe nor comfortable being a correspondent. A great part of the services were in supply and transport and office work. Even combat units got some rest after a mission was completed. But the war correspondents found that their papers got restive if they weren't near where things were happening. The result was that the correspondents had a very high casualty rate. If you stayed a correspondent long enough and went to the things that were happening, the chances were that you would get it. In reading these reports I am appalled at how many of the reporters are dead. Only a handful of the blithe spirits who made the nights horrible and filled the days with complaints, remain living.

But to get back to the conventions. It was the style to indicate that you were afraid all the time. I guess I was really afraid, but the style was there too. I think this was also designed to prove how brave the soldiers were. And the soldiers were just exactly as brave and as cowardly as anyone else.

We edited ourselves much more than we were edited. We felt responsible to what was called the home front. There was a general feeling that unless the home front was carefully protected from the whole account of what war was like, it might panic. Also we felt we had to protect the armed services from criticism, or they might retire to their tents to sulk like Achilles.

The self-discipline, self-censorship among the war correspondents was surely moral and patriotic but it was also practical in a sense of self-preservation. Some subjects were taboo. Certain people could not be criticized or even questioned. The foolish reporter who broke the rules would not be printed at home and in addition would be put out of the theater by the command, and a correspondent with no theater has no job.

We knew, for instance, that a certain very famous general officer constantly changed press agents because he felt he didn't get enough headlines. We knew the commander who broke a Signal Corps sergeant for photographing his wrong profile. Several fine field officers were removed from their commands by the jealousy of their superiors because they aroused too much enthusiasm in their men and too much admiration from the reporters. There were consistent sick leaves which were gigantic hangovers, spectacular liaisons between Army brass and WAACs, medical discharges for stupidity, brutality, cowardice, and even sex deviation. I don't know a single reporter who made use of any of this information. Apart from wartime morals, it would have been professional suicide to have done it. The one man who jumped the gun and scooped the world on the armistice was ruined in his profession, and his career was terminated.

Yes, we wrote only a part of the war, but at the time we believed, fervently believed, that it was the best thing to do. And perhaps that is why, when the war was over, novels and stories by ex-soldiers, like *The Naked and the Dead*, proved so shocking to a public which had been carefully protected from contact with the crazy hysterical mess.

We had plenty of material anyway. There was a super-abundance of heroism, selflessness, intelligence, and kindness to write about. And perhaps we were right in eliminating parts of the whole picture. Surely if we had sent all we knew, and couched in the language of the field, the home front would have been even more confused than we managed to make it. Besides, for every screaming egotist there was a Bradley, and for every publicity-mad military ham there were great men like Terry Allen and General Roosevelt, while in the ranks, billeted with the stinking, cheating, foul-mouthed goldbricks, there were true heroes, kindly men, intelligent men who knew or thought they knew what they were fighting for and took all the rest in their stride.

Professionally the war correspondents, I believe, were highly moral and responsible men, many of them very brave men, some of them completely dedicated men, but in the time after the story was filed I guess we were no better and no worse than the officers and enlisted men, only we had more facilities than the services, either commissioned or enlisted. We carried simulated ranks, ranging from captain to lieutenant colonel, which allowed us to eat at officers' mess, where enlisted men could not go, but we also had access to the enlisted men, where officers could not go. I remember an officers' dance in North Africa, a dull, cold little affair with junior officers mechanically dancing with commissioned nurses to old records on a wind-up phonograph, while in nearby barracks one of the finest jazz combos I ever heard was belting out pure ecstasy. Naturally we correspondents happily moved to the better music. Rank surely has its privileges, but with us it sometimes amounted to license. When our duty was done and our stories on the wire, we discovered and exchanged every address where black-market meat, liquor, and women could be procured. We knew the illegal taxis. We chiseled, stole, malingered, goldbricked, and generally made ourselves as comfortable as we could. I early learned that a pint of whisky to a transportation sergeant would get me on a plane ahead of a general with crash orders from the General Staff. We didn't steal much from the Army. We didn't have to. It was given to us. Besides we were up against experts in the Army. I remember a general in supply morosely reading a report of missing matériel from a supply depot and exploding, "The American soldier is the worst thief in the world. You know what's going to happen? When they steal everything we've got, they'll start stealing from the Germans, and then God help Hitler." And I remember on a destroyer at sea when every sidearm of every officer, 45s and carbines, suddenly disappeared, and although the ship was searched from stem to stern, even the fuel and water tanks explored, not one single weapon was ever found. There was a kind of a compulsion to steal. Prisoners were frisked for watches, cameras, and sidearms (the trade goods of the GIs) with professional skill. But the correspondents didn't steal much—first, as I said, because they didn't have to, and second, because we moved about so much that we couldn't take things with us. Heaven knows how many helmets, bedding rolls, and gas masks I was issued. I rarely got them where I was going, and I never got them back. In the cellars of London hotels today there must be trunks of loot left there fifteen years ago by correspondents and never claimed. I personally know of two such caches.

For what they are worth, or for what they may recapture, here they are, period pieces, fairy tales, half-meaningless memories of a time and of attitudes which have gone forever from the world, a sad and jocular recording of a little part of a war I saw and do not believe, unreal with trumped-up pageantry, so that it stands in the mind like the battle pictures of Crécy and Bunker Hill and Gettysburg. And, although all war is a symptom of man's failure as a thinking animal, still there was in these memory-wars some gallantry, some bravery, some kindliness. A man got killed, surely, or maimed, but, living, he did not carry crippled seed as a gift to his children.

Now for many years we have suckled on fear and fear alone, and there is no good product of fear. Its children are cruelty and deceit and suspicion germinating in our darkness. And just as surely as we are poisoning the air with our test bombs, so are we poisoned in our souls by fear, faceless, stupid sarcomic terror.

The pieces in this volume were written under pressure and in tension. My first impulse on rereading them was to correct, to change, to smooth out ragged sentences and remove repetitions, but their very raggedness is, it seems to me, a parcel of their immediacy. They are as real as the wicked witch and the good fairy, as true and tested and edited as any other myth.

There was a war, long ago—once upon a time.

England

*　　*

TROOPSHIP

Somewhere in England, *June 20, 1943*—The troops in their thousands sit on their equipment on the dock. It is evening, and the first of the dimout lights come on. The men wear their helmets, which make them all look alike, make them look like long rows of mushrooms. Their rifles are leaning against their knees. They have no identity, no personality. The men are units in an army. The numbers chalked on their helmets are almost like the license numbers on robots. Equipment is piled neatly—bedding rolls and half-shelters and barracks bags. Some of the men are armed with Springfield or Enfield rifles from the First World War, some with M-1s, or Garands, and some with the neat, light clever little carbines everyone wants to have after the war for hunting rifles.

Above the pier the troopship rears high and thick as an office building. You have to crane your neck upward to see where the portholes stop and the open decks begin. She is a nameless ship and will be while the war lasts. Her destination is known to very few men and her route to even fewer, and the burden of the men who command her must be almost unendurable, for the master who loses her and her cargo will never sleep comfortably again. He probably doesn't sleep at all now. The cargo holds are loaded and the ship waits to take on her tonnage of men.

On the dock the soldiers are quiet. There is little talking, no singing, and as dusk settles to dark you cannot tell one man from another. The heads bend forward with weariness. Some of these men have been all day, some many days, getting to this starting point.

There are several ways of wearing a hat or a cap. A man may express himself in the pitch or tilt of his hat, but not with a helmet. There is only one way to wear a helmet. It won't go on any other way. It sits level on the head, low over eyes and ears, low on the back of the neck. With your helmet on you are a mushroom in a bed of mushrooms.

Four gangways are open now and the units get wearily to their feet and shuffle along in line. The men lean forward against the weight of their equipment. Feet drag against the incline of the gangways. The soldiers disappear one by one into the great doors in the side of the troopship.

Inside the checkers tabulate them. The numbers chalked on the helmets are checked again against a list. Places have been assigned. Half of the men will sleep on the decks and the other half inside in ballrooms, in dining rooms where once a very different kind of people sat and found very important things that have disappeared. Some of the men will sleep in bunks, in hammocks, on the deck, in passages. Tomorrow they will shift. The men from the deck will come in to sleep and those from inside will go out. They will change every night until they land. They will not take off their clothes until they land. This is no cruise ship.

On the decks, dimmed to a faint blue dusk by the blackout lights, the men sink down and fall asleep. They are asleep almost as soon as they are settled. Many of them do not even take off their helmets. It has been a weary day. The rifles are beside them, held in their hands.

On the gangways the lines still feed into the troopship— a regiment of colored troops, a hundred Army nurses, neat in their helmets and field packs. The nurses at least will have staterooms, however crowded they may be in them. Up No. 1 Gangway comes the headquarters complement of a bombardment wing and a company of military police. All are equally tired. They find their places and go to sleep.

Embarkation is in progress. No smoking is allowed anywhere. Everyone entering the ship is triply checked, to make sure he belongs there, and the loading is very quiet. There is only the shuffle of tired feet on the stairways and quiet orders. The permanent crew of military police know every move. They have handled this problem of traffic before.

The tennis courts on the upper deck are a half-acre of sleeping men now—men, feet, and equipment. MPs are everywhere, on stairs and passages, directing and watching. This embarkation must go on smoothly, for one little block might well lose hours in the loading, just as one willful driver, making a wrong turn in traffic, may jam an avenue for a long time. But in spite of the shuffling gait, the embarkation is very rapid. About midnight the last man is aboard.

In the staff room the commanding officer sits behind a long

table, with telephones in front of him. His adjutant, a tired blond major, makes his report and places his papers on the table. The CO nods and gives him an order.

Throughout the ship the loudspeakers howl. Embarkation is complete. The gangways slide down from the ship. The iron doors close. No one can enter or leave the ship now, except the pilot. On the bridge the captain of the ship paces slowly. It is his burden now. These thousands are in his care, and if there is an accident it will be his blame.

The ship remains against the pier and a light breathing sound comes from deep in her. The troops are cut off now and gone from home, although they are not a hundred steps from home. On the upper decks a few men lean over the rails and look down on the pier and away at the city behind. The oily water ripples with the changing tide. It is almost time to go. In the staff room, which used to be the ship's theater, the commanding officer sits behind his table. His tired, blond adjutant sits beside him. The phone rings, the CO picks it up, listens for a moment and hangs up the receiver. He turns to the adjutant.

"All ready," he says.

* *

SOMEWHERE IN ENGLAND, *June 21, 1943*—The tide is turning now and it is after midnight. On the bridge, which towers above the pier buildings, there is great activity. The lines are cast off and the engines reversed. The great ship backs carefully into the stream and nearly fills it to both banks. But the little tugs are waiting for her and they bump and persuade her about until she is headed right and they hang beside her like suckling ships as she moves slowly toward the sea. Only the MPs on watch among the sleeping soldiers see the dimmed-out city slipping by.

Down deep in the ship, in the hospital, the things that can happen to so many men have started to happen. A medical major has taken off his blouse and rolled up his sleeves. He is washing his hands in green soap, while an Army nurse in operating uniform stands by, holding the doctor's white gown. The anonymous soldier, with the dangerous appendix, is having his stomach shaved by another Army nurse. Brilliant light floods the operating table. The doctor major slips into his sterile gloves. The nurse adjusts the mask over his nose and mouth and he steps quickly to the sleeping soldier on the table under the light.

The great troopship sneaks past the city and the tugs leave her, a dark thing steaming into the dark. On the decks and in the passages and in the bunks the thousands of men are collapsed in sleep. Only their faces show under the dim blue blackout lights—faces and an impression of tangled hands and feet and legs and equipment. Officers and military police stand guard over this great sleep, a sleep multiplied, the sleep of thousands. An odor rises from the men, the character-istic odor of an army. It is the smell of wool and the bitter smell of fatigue and the smell of gun oil and leather. Troops always have this odor. The men lie sprawled, some with their mouths open, but they do not snore. Perhaps they are too tired to snore, but their breathing is a pulsing, audible thing.

The tired blond adjutant haunts the deck like a ghost. He doesn't know when he will ever sleep again. He and the provost marshal share responsibility for a smooth crossing, and both are serious and responsible men.

The sleeping men are missing something tremendous, as last things are usually missed. The clerks and farmers, sales-men, students, laborers, technicians, reporters, fishermen who have stopped being those things to become an army have been trained from their induction for this moment. This is the beginning of the real thing for which they have prac-ticed. Their country, which they have become soldiers to defend, is slipping away into the misty night and they are asleep. The place which will fill their thoughts in the months to come is gone and they did not see it go. They were asleep.

They will not see it again for a long time, and some of them will never see it again. This was the time of emotion, the moment that cannot be replaced, but they were too tired. They sleep like children who really tried to stay awake to see Santa Claus and couldn't make it. They will remember this time, but it will never really have happened to them.

The night begins to come in over the sea. It is overcast and a light rain begins to fall. It is good sailing weather because a submarine could not see us 200 yards away. The ship is a gray, misty shape, slipping through a gray mist and melting into it. Overhead a Navy blimp watches over her, sometimes coming in so close that you can see the men in the little underslung cabin.

The troopship is cut off now. She can hear but cannot speak. Her outgoing radio will not be used at all unless she is hit or attacked. For the time of her voyage no one will hear of her. Submarines are in the misty sea ahead, and of the men on board very many have never seen the ocean before and the sea itself is dark and terrifying enough without the lurking things, and there are other matters besides the future fighting that frighten a local boy—new things, new people, new languages.

The men are beginning to awaken now, before the call. They have missed the moment of parting. They awaken to —destination unknown, route unknown, life even for an hour ahead unknown. The great ship throws her bow into the Atlantic.

On the boat deck two early-rising mountain boys are standing, looking in wonder at the incredible sea. One of them says, "They say she's salty clear down to the bottom."

"Now you know that ain't so," the other says.

"What you mean, it ain't so? Why ain't it so?"

The other speaks confidently. "Now, son," he says, "you know there ain't that much salt in the world. Just figure it out for yourself."

*   *

SOMEWHERE IN ENGLAND, *June 22, 1943*—The first morning on a troopship is a mess. The problem of feeding thousands of men in such close quarters is profound. There are two meals a day, spaced ten hours apart. Mess lines for breakfast form at seven and continue until ten. Dinner lines start at five in the afternoon and continue until ten at night. And during these times the long, narrow corridors are lined with men, three abreast, carrying their field kits.

On the first day the system does not take effect. There are traffic jams and thin tempers. At ten in the morning a miserable private in chemical warfare whines to a military policeman, who is keeping the lines shuffling along. "Please, mister. Get me out of this line. I have had three breakfasts already. I ain't hungry no more. Every time I get out of one line I get shoved into another one."

Men cannot be treated as individuals on this troopship.

They are simply units which take up six feet by three feet by two feet, horizontal or vertical. So much space must be allotted for the physical unit. They are engines which must be given fuel to keep them from stopping. The products of their combustion must be taken care of and eliminated. There is no way of considering them as individuals. The second and third day the method begins to work. The line flows smoothly and on time, but that first day is a mess.

The men are rested now and there is no room to move about. They will not be able to have any exercise during this voyage. There are too many feet. The major impression on a troop ship is of feet. A man can get his head out of the way and his arms, but, lying or sitting, his feet are a problem. They sprawl in the aisles, they stick up at all angles. They are not protected because they are the part of a man least likely to be hurt. To move about you must step among feet, must trip over feet.

There are big, misshapen feet; neat, small feet; shoes that are polished; curl-toed shoes; shoestrings knotted and snarled, and careful little bows. You can read character by the feet and shoes. There are perpetually tired feet, and nervous, quick feet. To remember a troopship is to remember feet. At night on a blacked-out ship, you must creep and feel your way among acres of feet.

The men begin to be restless now. It is hard to sit still and do nothing. Some have brought the little pocket books and others go to the ship's library and get books. Detective stories and short stories. They take what they can get. But there are many men who do not consider reading a matter of pleasure and these must find some other outlet for their interests.

Several months ago Services of Supply, in reporting the

items supplied to the soldiers' exchanges, included several hundreds of thousands of sets of dice, explaining that parcheesi was becoming increasingly popular in the Army. Those who remember parcheesi as a rather dumpy game may not believe this if they have not seen it, but it is so. The game has been streamlined to a certain extent but there is no doubt of its popularity. The board with its string pockets has disappeared in the interest of space. Parcheesi is now played on an Army blanket.

It is a spirited, healthy game, and seems to hold the attention of the players. Some tournaments of parcheesi continue for days. One, indeed, never stopped during the whole crossing. Another game which is very popular in the Army is cassino. Its most common forms are stud cassino and five-card-draw cassino. It is gratifying to see that our new Army has gone back to the old-fashioned virtues our forefathers lied about.

The ship is very heavily armed. From every point of observation the guns protrude. This troopship could fight her way through considerable opposition. On the decks, in addition to the lifeboats, are hundreds of life rafts ready to be thrown into the sea. These boats and rafts are equipped with food and water and medicine and even fishing tackle.

Now the men who slept on the decks last night move inside, as the inside men move out. The wind is fresh. The soldiers take out the shelter halves and begin to build ingenious shelters. Some erect single little covers between stanchions and rails, while others, pooling their canvas, are able to make windproof caves among the life rafts. In these they settle down to read or to play parcheesi or cassino. The sea is calm and that is good, for great numbers of the men have never been on any kind of boat. A little rough weather will make them seasick and then there will be an added problem for the worried and tired permanent force on the boat.

The decks cannot be flushed, for there is no place for the men to go while it is being done. There are many delicate problems on such a ship. If another ship should be sighted, the men must not crowd to one side, for that would throw too great a weight on one side of the ship and might even endanger her. Our cargo is men and it must be shifted with care.

Every day there is boat drill. The alarm sounds, and after the first day of pandemonium the men go quietly to their stations. There are so many problems to be faced on a troopship.

*　　　*

SOMEWHERE IN ENGLAND, *June 23, 1943*—A troopship is a strange community and it reacts as a community. It is unique, however, in that it is cut off from all the world and that it is in constant danger of being attacked and destroyed. No matter how casual the men seem, that last fact is never very far from their minds. In the water any place may be the submarine and any moment may come the blast that sends the great ship to the bottom.

Thus the gunners never relax, the listening devices are tense and occupied. Half the mind listens and waits all the time and in the night small sounds take on a large importance. At intervals the guns are fired to see that they are in perfect condition. The gunnery officer never relaxes. On the bridge the captain sleeps very rarely and takes his coffee in his hand.

Under such a strain the human brain reacts curiously. It builds its apprehensions into realities and then repeats those realities. Thus a troopship is a nest of rumors, rumors that go whisking from stem to stern, but the most curious thing is that on all troopships the rumors are the same. Some generalized picture takes shape in all of them. The story starts and is repeated, and everyone, except perhaps the permanent crew, believes each rumor for a few hours before a new one takes its place. It might be well to set down some of these rumors so that when heard they will be recognized for what they are, the folklore of a troopship.

The following are heard on every troopship, without exception; further, they are believed on every troopship:

1. This morning we were sighted by a submarine. It could not catch us, but it radioed its fellows and now a pack is assembling ahead of us to intercept us and sink us. This rumor is supposed to come from the radio officer, who heard the submarine calling its brothers. The pack will close in on us tonight. All of these rumors are said to come from a responsible officer.

2. This morning a submarine surfaced, not knowing we were near. We had every gun trained on her, ready to blow her out of the water, because we heard her in our listening devices. She saw us as she broke water and signaled just in time that she was one of ours. It is not explained how it happens that

she did not hear us in her listening devices, and if the question arises it is explained that probably her listening devices were out of order.

3. Some terrible and nameless thing has happened among the officers (this rumor is only among the enlisted men). The crime they have committed is not mentioned, but it is known that a number of officers are under detention and will be court-martialed. This rumor may be pure wishful thinking.

4. Both the officers' post exchanges and the enlisted men's post exchanges sell a water pop in brown bottles. The soldiers know very well that what is in their bottles is pop, but the rumor runs through the ship that the brown bottles in the officers' lounge contain beer. Some little discontent arises from this until it is forgotten in a new rumor.

5. The front end of the ship is weak and only patched up. On the last voyage she cut a destroyer (sometimes a cruiser) in two and they patched her up and sent her out anyway. She is perfectly all right, unless we run into heavy weather, in which case she is very likely to fall to pieces. Since men are not allowed on the forepeak, because the gun crews are there, they cannot look over and see whether or not this is true.

6. Last night the German radio announced that this ship had been sunk. The Germans often do this, fishing for information. While parents, wives, and friends do not know exactly what ship we are on, they know about when we were alerted and they will be frantic and there is no way of telling them that we are all right, for no messages are permitted to go out. The soldiers go about worrying to think of the worry of their people.

7. Some kind of epidemic has broken out on the ship. The officers are keeping it quiet to prevent a panic. They are burying the dead secretly at night.

As the days go by and the men grow more restless and the parcheesi games have fallen off because the sinews of the game have got into a few lean and hungry hands, the rumors grow more intense. Somewhere in mid-ocean a big patrol plane flies near to us and circles protectively, and the rumor springs up that she has signaled the captain to change course. Something terrific is going on somewhere and we are changing our destination.

Since we change our course every thirty seconds anyway, there is no telling by watching the wake where we are going. So the rumors go. It would be interesting if the ship's officers would post a list of rumors the men are likely to hear. It would certainly eliminate some apprehensions on the part of the men, and it would be interesting to see whether then a whole new list of fresh, unused rumors would grow up.

*　　　*

SOMEWHERE IN ENGLAND, *June 24, 1943*—A small USO unit is aboard this troopship, girls and men who are going out to entertain troops wherever they may be sent.

These are not the big names who go out with blasts of publicity and maintain their radio contracts. These are girls who can sing and dance and look pretty and men who can do magic and pantomimists and tellers of jokes. They have few properties and none of the tricks of light and color which dress up the theater. But there is something very gallant about them. The theater is the only institution in the world which has been dying for four thousand years and has never succumbed. It requires tough and devoted people to keep it alive. An accordion is the largest piece of property the troupe carries. The evening dresses, crushed in suitcases, must be pressed and kept pretty. The spirit must be high. This is trouping the really hard way.

The theater is one of the largest mess halls. Soldiers are packed in, sitting on benches, standing on tables, lying in the doorways. A little platform on one end is the stage. To-night the loudspeaker is out of order, but when it isn't it blares and distorts voices. The master of ceremonies gets up and faces his packed audience. He tells a joke—but this audience is made up of men from different parts of the country and each part has its own kind of humor. He tells a New York joke. There is a laugh, but a limited one. The men from South Dakota and Oklahoma do not understand this joke. They laugh late, merely because they want to laugh. He tries another joke and this time he plays safe. It is an Army joke about MPs. This time it works. Everybody likes a joke about MPs.

He introduces an acrobatic dancer, a pretty girl with long legs and the strained smile acrobats develop to conceal the fact that their muscles are crying with tension. The ship is rolling slowly from side to side. All of her work is dependent on perfect balance. She tries each part of her act several times and is thrown off balance, but, seriously, she tries again until, in a pause in the ship's roll she succeeds, and legs are distorted properly for the proper two seconds. The soldiers are with her. They know the difficulty. They want her to succeed and they cheer when she does. This is all very serious. She leaves the stage under whistles and cheers.

A blues singer follows. Without the loudspeaker she can hardly be heard, for her voice, although sweet, has no volume. She forces her voice for volume and loses her sweetness, but she is pretty and young and earnest.

A girl accordion-player comes next. She asks for suggestions. This is to be group singing and the requests are for old songs—"Harvest Moon," "Home on the Range," "When Irish Eyes Are Smiling." The men bellow the words in all pitches. There is no war song for this war. Nothing has come along yet. The show continues—a pantomimist who acts out the physical examination of an inductee and does it so accurately that his audience howls. A magician in traditional tail coat manipulates colored silks.

In all the acts the illusion does not quite come off. The audience helps all it can because it wants the show to be good. And out of the little acts, which are not quite convincing, and the big audience which wants literally to be convinced, something whole and good comes, so that when it is over there has been a show.

One of the men in the unit has been afraid. He has not slept since the ship sailed. He is afraid of the ocean and of submarines. He has lain in his bunk, listening for the blast that will kill him. He is probably very brave. He does his act when he is terrified. It is foolish to say he should not be afraid. He is afraid, and that is something he cannot control, but he does his act, and that is something he can control.

Up on the deck in the blackness the colored troops are sprawled. They sit quietly. A great bass voice sings softly a bar of the hymn "When the Saints Go Marching In." A voice says, "Sing it, brother!"

The bass takes it again and a few other voices join him. By the time the hymn has reached the fourth bar an organ of voices is behind it. The voices take on a beat, feeling one another out. The chords begin to form. There is nothing visible. The booming voices come out of the darkness. The men sing sprawled out, lying on their backs. The song becomes huge with authority. This is a war song. This could be *the* war song. Not the sentimental wash about lights coming on again or bluebirds.

The black deck rolls with sound. One chorus ends and another starts, "When the Saints Go Marching In." Four times and on the fifth the voices fade away to a little hum and the deck is silent again. The ship rolls and metal protests against metal. The ship is silent again. Only the shudder of the engine and the whisk of water and the whine of the wind in the wire rigging break the silence.

We have not yet a singing Army nor any songs for a singing Army. Synthetic emotions and nostalgias do not take hold because the troops know instinctively that they are synthetic. No one has yet put words and a melody to the real homesickness, the real terror, and the real ferocity of the war.

*   *

SOMEWHERE IN ENGLAND, *June 25, 1943*—We are coming close to land. The birds picked us up this morning and a big flying boat circled us and then darted away to report us. There has been no trouble at all, and if, on the bridge, the enemy has been reported, we do not know it. The word sifts down from the bridge that we shall land tonight. The soldiers line the rails and report every low-hanging cloud as a landfall. Now that we are near and the lines of our approach are narrow, the danger is greater. The ship swerves and turns constantly. These waters are the most dangerous of all.

The men are reading a little booklet that has been distributed, telling them how to get along with the English. The book explains language differences. It suggests that in England a closet is not a place to hang clothing, that the word "bloody" should be avoided, that a garbage can is a dust bin, and it warns that the English use many common words with a meaning different from what we assign to them. Many of our men find this very funny and they go about talking a curious gibberish which they imagine is a British accent.

A light haze shrouds the horizon, and out of it our Spitfires drive at us and circle like angry bees. They come so close that we hear the fierce whistle of their wings. For a long time they circle us and then go away, and others take their place.

In the afternoon land shows through the haze and, as we get closer, the neat houses and the neat country, orderly and old. The men gaze at it in wonder. It is the first foreign place most of them have ever seen and each man says it looks like some place he knows. One says it looks like California in the spring-time of a wet year. Another recognizes Vermont. The men crowd to the portholes and the rails.

The troopship moves into a harbor and drops her anchor. She is surrounded on all sides by shipping and by naval units. The men will go ashore in lighters, but not yet, for disembarkation is, if anything, more complicated than embarkation. Men can easily be lost or mixed with the wrong units.

The night comes and in the staff room the officers gather and wait until they are assigned the transportation for their men. It takes a good part of the night. At an exact time each unit must be in an exact place, where a lighter will be waiting to take them on. The troop trains will be waiting ashore. It has been a perfect crossing. No trouble, no sickness, no attack. The ship's officers show the strain. They haven't slept much. After a few voyages they must be relieved. The responsibilty is too great for a man to bear for too long a stretch.

In the morning the lighters come in and hug the sides of the troopship. The big iron doors open and the troops move out and take their places on the decks of the little boats. The port-holes high above are filled with heads looking down. Men for a later debarkation. The little boat moves off, puffs up the bay among the tugs and the destroyers and the anchored freighters. The soldiers are self-conscious in a new place. They regard this new land skeptically as one must when he is not sure of himself. The little boat puffs up to the dock, which has mysteriously become a quay, pronounced "key," which is, of course, ridiculous.

Now as the lighter ties up an astonishing thing happens. A band of pipers marches out in kilts, with bagpipes and drums and the swingy march of pipers. The harsh skirling cuts through the air. The most military, the most fighting music in the world. Our men crowd the rail. The band approaches, drums banging, pipes squealing and, as they draw abreast, the soldiers break into a great cheer. They may not like the harsh music; it takes time to like it; but something of the iron of the music goes into them. The pipers wheel and march back and away. It was a good thing to do. Our men, in some deep way, feel honored. The music has stirred them. This is a different war from the one of training camps and strategy at post exchanges.

From the deck of the lighter the men can see the roofless houses, the burned-out houses. The piles of rubble where the bombs have fallen. They have seen pictures of this and have read about it, but that was pictures and reading. It wasn't real. This is different. It isn't like the pictures at all. On the quay, the Red Cross is waiting with caldrons of coffee, with mountains of cake. They have been serving since dawn and they will serve until long after dark. The gangplank to the lighter is fixed now. The men, carrying their heavy barrack bags, packs on their backs and rifles slung over their shoulders, struggle up the steep gangway to the new country. And in the distance they can hear the sound of the pipes greeting another lighter-load of troops.

*　　　*

A PLANE'S NAME

A BOMBER STATION, *June 26, 1943*—The bomber crew is getting back from London. The men have been on a forty-eight-hour pass. At the station an Army bus is waiting, and they pile in with other crews. Then the big bus moves through the narrow streets of the little ancient town and rolls into the pleasant green country. Fields of wheat with hedge-rows between. On the right is one of the huge vegetable gardens all cut up into little plots where families raise their own produce. Some men and women are working in the garden now, having ridden out of town on their bicycles.

The Army bus rattles over the rough road and through a patch of woods. In the distance there are a few squat brown buildings and a flagstaff flying the American flag. This is a bomber station. England is littered with them. This is one of the best. There is no mud here, and the barracks are permanent and adequate. There is no high concentration of planes in any one field. Probably no more than twenty-five Flying Fortresses live here, and they are so spread out that you do not see them at once. A raider might get one of them, but he would not be likely to get more than one.

No attempt is made to camouflage the buildings or the planes—it doesn't work and it's just a lot of work. Air protection and dispersal do work. Barbed wire is strung along the road, coils of it, and in front of the administration building there is a gate with a sentry box. The bus pulls to a stop near the gate and the men jump down, adjusting their gas masks at their sides. No one is permitted to leave the place without his gas mask. The men file through the gate, identify themselves, and sign in back on the post. The crews walk slowly to their barracks.

The room is long and narrow and unpainted. Against each side wall are iron double-decker bunks, alternating with clothes lockers. A long rack in the middle between the bunks serves as a hanger for winter coats and raincoats. Next to it is the rack of rifles and submachine guns of the crew.

Each bunk is carefully made, and to the foot of each are hung a helmet and a gas mask. On the walls are pin-up girls. But the same girls near each bunk—big-breasted blondes in languorous attitudes, child faces, parted shiny lips and sleepy eyes, which doubtless mean passion, but always the same girls.

The crew of the *Mary Ruth* have their bunks on the right-hand side of the room. They have had these bunks only a few weeks. A Fortress was shot down and the bunks were emptied. It is strange to sleep in the bed of a man who was at breakfast with you and now is dead or a prisoner hundreds of miles away. It is strange and necessary. His clothes are in the locker, to be picked up and put away. His helmet is to be taken off the foot of the bunk and yours put there. You leave his pin-up girls where they are. Why change them? Yours would be the same girls.

This crew did not name or come over in the *Mary Ruth*. On the nose of the ship her name is written, and under it "Memories of Mobile." But this crew does not know who Mary Ruth was, nor what memories are celebrated. She was named when they got her, and they would not think of changing her name. In some way it would be bad luck.

A rumor has swept through the airfields that some powerful group in America has protested about the names of the ships and that an order is about to be issued removing these names and substituting the names of towns and rivers. It is to be hoped that this is not true. Some of the best writing of the war has been on the noses of bombers. The names are highly personal things, and the ships grow to be people. Change the name of *Bomb Boogie* to *St. Louis*, or *Mary Ruth* of Mobile Memories to *Wichita*, or the *Volga Virgin* to *Davenport*, and you will have injured the ship. The name must be perfect and must be approved by every member of the crew. The names must not be changed. There is enough dullness in the war as it is.

Mary Ruth's crew sit on their bunks and discuss the hard luck of *Bomb Boogie*. *Bomb Boogie* is a hard-luck ship. She never gets to her target. Every mission is an abortion. They bring her in and go over her and test her and take her on test runs. She is perfect and then she starts on an operational flight, and her engines go bad or her landing gear gives trouble. Something always happens to *Bomb Boogie*. She never gets to her target. It is something no one can understand. Four days ago she started out and never got as far as the coast of England before one of her engines conked out and she had to return.

One of the waist gunners strolls out, but in a minute he is back. "We're alerted for tomorrow," he says. "I hope it isn't Kiel. There was a hell of a lot of red flak at Kiel."

"The guy with the red beard is there," says Brown, the tail gunner. "He looked right at me. I drew down on him and my guns jammed."

"Let's go eat," the turret gunner says.

*   *

NEWS FROM HOME

BOMBER STATION IN ENGLAND, *June 28, 1943*—The days are very long. A combination of summer time and day-light-saving time keeps them light until eleven-thirty. After mess we take the Army bus into town. It is an ancient little city which every American knows about as soon as he can read. The buildings on the narrow streets are Tudor, Stuart, Georgian, and even some Norman. The paving stones are worn smooth and the flagstones of the sidewalks are grooved by ages of strollers. It is a town to stroll in. American soldiers, Canadians, Royal Air Force men, and many of Great Britain's women soldiers walk through the streets. But Britain drafts its women and they are really in the Army, driver-mechanics, dispatch riders, trim and hard in their uniforms.

The crew of the *Mary Ruth* ends up at a little pub, over-crowded and noisy. They edge their way in to the bar, where the barmaids are drawing beer as fast as they can. In a moment this crew has found a table and they have the small glasses of pale yellow fluid in front of them. It is curious beer. Most of the alcohol has been taken out of it to make munitions. It is not cold. It is token beer—a gesture rather than a drink.

The bomber crew is solemn. Men who are alerted for operational missions are usually solemn, but tonight there is some burden on this crew. There is no way of knowing how these things start. All at once a crew will feel fated. Then little things go wrong. Then they are uneasy until they take off for their mission. When the uneasiness is running it is the waiting that hurts.

They sip the flat, tasteless beer. One of them says, "I saw a paper from home at the Red Cross in London." It is quiet. The others look at him across their glasses. A mixed group of pilots and ATS girls at the other end of the pub have started a song. It is astonishing how many of the songs are American. "You'd Be So Nice to Come Home to," they sing. And the beat of the song is subtly changed. It has become an English song.

The waist gunner raises his voice to be heard over the singing. "It seems to me that we are afraid to announce our losses. It seems almost as if the War Department was afraid that the country couldn't take it. I never saw anything the country couldn't take."

The ball-turret gunner wipes his mouth with the back of his hand. "We don't hear much," he says, "it's a funny thing, but the closer you get to action the less you read papers and war news. I remember before I joined up I used to know everything that was happening. I knew what Turkey was doing. I

27

even had maps with pins and I drew out campaigns with colored pencils. Now I haven't looked at a paper in two weeks."

The first man went on, "This paper I saw had some funny stuff in it. It seemed to think that the war was nearly over."

"I wish the Jerries thought that," the tail gunner says. "I wish you could get Goering's yellow noses and them damned flak gunners convinced of that."

"Well anyway," the waist gunner says, "I looked through that paper pretty close. It seems to me that the folks at home are fighting one war and we're fighting another one. They've got theirs nearly won and we've just got started on ours. I wish they'd get in the same war we're in. I wish they'd print the casualties and tell them what it's like. I think maybe that they'd like to get in the same war we're in if they could get it to do."

The tail gunner comes from so close to the border of Kentucky he talks like a Kentuckian. "I read a very nice piece in a magazine about us," he says. "This piece says we've got nerves of steel. We never get scared. All we want in the world is just to fly all the time and get a crack at Jerry. I never heard anything so brave as us. I read it three or four times to try and convince myself that I ain't scared."

"There was almost solid red flak over Bremen last Thursday," the radio man says. "Get much more and we can walk home over solid flak. I hate that red flak. We sure took a pasting Thursday."

"Well, we didn't get any," says Henry Maurice Crain, one of the gunners. "We got the nose knocked out of our ship, but that was an accident. One of the gunners in a ship high on ahead tossed out some shell casings and they came right through the nose. They've got her nearly fixed up now."

"But anyway," the first man says doggedly, "I wish they'd tell them at home that the war isn't over and I wish they wouldn't think we're so brave. I don't want to be so brave. Shall we have another beer?"

"What for?" says the tail gunner. "This stuff hasn't got even enough character for you to dislike it. I'm going back to wipe my guns. Then I won't have to do it in the morning."

They stand up and file slowly out of the pub. It is still daylight. The pigeons are flying about the tower of an old Gothic church, a kind of architecture especially suited to nesting pigeons.

The hotel taken over by the Red Cross is crowded with men in from the flying fields which dot the countryside. Our bus drives up in front and we pile in. The crew looks automatically at the sky. It is clear, with little puffs of white cloud suspended in the light of a sun that has already gone down.

"Looks like it might be a clear day," the radio man says. "That's good for us and it's good for them to get at us."

The bus rattles back toward the field. The tail gunner muses. "I hope old Red Beard has got a bad cold," he says. "I didn't like the look in his eye last time."

(Red Beard is an enemy fighter pilot who comes so close that you can almost see his face.)

*   *

SUPERSTITION

BOMBER STATION IN ENGLAND, *June 30, 1943*—It is a
bad night in the barracks, such a night as does not happen very
often. It is impossible to know how it starts. Nerves are a little
thin and no one is sleepy. The tail gunner of the other outfit in
the room gets down from his upper bunk and begins rooting
about on the floor.

"What's the matter?" the man on the lower bunk asks.

"I lost my medallion," the tail gunner says.

No one asks what it was, a St. Christopher or a good-luck
piece. The fact of the matter is that it is his medallion and he
has lost it. Everyone gets up and looks. They move the double-
decker bunk out from the wall. They empty all the shoes.
They look behind the steel lockers. They insist that the gunner go through all his pockets. It isn't a good thing for a man
to lose his medallion. Perhaps there has been an uneasiness before. This sets it. The uneasiness creeps all through the room.
It takes the channel of being funny. They tell jokes; they rag

one another. They ask shoe sizes of one another to outrage their uneasiness. "What size shoes you wear, Brown? I get them if you conk out." The thing runs bitterly through the room.

And then the jokes stop. There are many little things you do when you go out on a mission. You leave the things that are to be sent home if you have an accident. You leave them under your pillow, your photographs and the letter you wrote, and your ring. They're under your pillow, and you don't make up your bunk. That must be left unmade so that you can slip right in when you get back. No one would think of making up a bunk while its owner is on a mission. You go out clean-shaven too, because you are coming back, to keep your date. You project your mind into the future and the things you are going to do then.

In the barracks they tell of presentiments they have heard about. There was the radio man who one morning folded his bedding neatly on his cot and put his pillow on top. And he folded his clothing into a neat parcel and cleared his locker. He had never done anything like that before. And sure enough, he was shot down that day.

The tail gunner still hasn't found his medallion. He has gone through his pockets over and over again. The brutal talk goes on until one voice says, "For God's sake shut up. It's after midnight. We've got to get some sleep."

The lights are turned out. It is pitch black in the room, for the blackout curtains are drawn tight. A man speaks in the darkness. "I wish I was in that ship by now." He knows that he will be all right when the mission starts. It's this time of waiting that hurts, and tonight it has been particularly bad.

It is quiet in the room, and then there is a step, and then a

31

great clatter. A new arrival trying to get to his bunk in the dark has stumbled over the gun rack. The room breaks into loud curses. Everyone curses the new arrival. They tell him where he came from and where they hope he will go. It is a fine, noisy outburst, and the tension goes out of the room. The evil thing has gone.

You are conscious, lying in your bunk, of a droning sound that goes on and on. It is the Royal Air Force going out for the night bombing again. There must be hundreds of them— a big raid. The sound has been going on all evening and it goes on for another hour. Hundreds of Lancasters, with hundreds of tons of bombs. And, when they come back, you will go out.

You cannot call the things that happen to bombing crews superstition. Tension and altitude do strange things to a man. At 30,000 feet, the body is living in a condition it was not born to withstand. A man is breathing oxygen from a tube and his eyes and ears are working in the reduced pressure. It is little wonder, then, that he sometimes sees things that are not there and does not see things that are there. Gunners have fired on their own ships and others have poured great bursts into empty air, thinking they saw a swastika. The senses are not trustworthy. And the sky is treacherous with flak. The flak bursts about you and sometimes the fragments come tearing through your ship. The fighters stab past you, flaring with their guns. And, if you happen to see little visions now and then, why, that's bound to happen. And if on your intensified awareness, small incidents are built up with meanings, why, such things always happen under tension. Ghosts have always ridden through skies and if your body and nerves are strained with altitude, too, such things are bound to happen.

The barrack room is very silent. From a corner comes a light snore. Someone is talking in his sleep. First a sentence mumbled and then, "Helen, let's go in the Ferris wheel now."

There is secret sound from the far wall, and then a tiny clink of metal. The tail gunner is still feeling through his pockets for his medallion.

*   *

PREPARATION FOR A RAID

BOMBER STATION IN ENGLAND, *July 1, 1943*—In the barracks, a brilliant white light flashes on, jerking you out of sleep. A sharp voice says, "All right, get out of it! Briefing at three o'clock, stand-by at four-twenty. Better get out of it now."

The crew struggles sleepily out of their bunks and into clothes. It is 2:30 a.m. There hasn't been much sleep for anyone.

Outside the daylight is beginning to come. The crew gropes its way through sleepiness and the semidarkness to the guarded door, and each goes in as he is recognized by the guard.

Inside there are rows of benches in front of a large white screen, which fills one wall. Some of the crews are already seated. The lights go out and from a projector an aerial photograph is projected on the screen. It is remarkably clear. It shows streets and factories and a winding river, and docks and submarine pens. An Intelligence officer stands beside the screen and he holds a long pointer in his hand. He begins without preliminary. "Here is where you are going," he says, and he names a German city.

"Now this squadron will come in from this direction," the pointer traces the road, making a black shadow on the screen. The pointer stops at three long, narrow buildings, side by side. "This is your target. They make small engine parts here. Knock it out." He mentions times and as he does a sergeant marks the times on a blackboard. "Stand-by at such a time, take-off at such a time. You will be over your target at such a time, and you should be back here by such a time." It is all on the minute—5:52 and 9:43. The incredible job of getting so many ships to a given point at a given time means almost split-second timing.

The Intelligence officer continues: (Next three sentences cut by censor.) "Good luck and good hunting." The lights flood on. The pictured city disappears. A chaplain comes to the front of the room. "All Catholics gather at the back of the room," he says.

The crews straggle across the way to the mess hall and fill their plates and their cups, stewed fruit and scrambled eggs and bacon and cereal and coffee.

The *Mary Ruth's* crew is almost gay. It is a reaction to the bad time they had the night before. All of the tension is broken now, for there is work and flying to be done, not waiting. The tail gunner says, "If anything should happen today, I want to go on record that I had prunes for breakfast."

They eat hurriedly and then file out, washing their dishes and cups in soapy water and then rinsing them in big caldrons near the door.

Dressing is a long and complicated business. The men strip to the skin. Next to their skins they put on long light woolen underwear. Over that they slip on what looks like long light-blue-colored underwear, but these are the heated suits. They come low on the ankles and far down on the wrists, and from the waists of these suits protrude electric plugs. The suit, between two layers of fabric, is threaded with electric wires which will carry heat when the plug is connected to the heat outlet on the ship. Over the heated suit goes the brown coverall. Last come thick, fleece-lined heated boots and gloves which also have plugs for the heat unit. Next goes on the Mae West, the orange rubber life preserver, which can be inflated in a moment. Then comes the parachute with its heavy canvas straps over the shoulders and between the legs. And last the helmet with the throat speaker and the earphones attached. Plugged in to the intercommunications system, the man can now communicate with the rest of the crew no matter what noise is going on about him. During the process the men have got bigger and bigger as layer on layer of equipment is put on. They walk stiffly, like artificial men. The lean waist gunner is now a little chubby.

They dress very carefully, for an exposed place or a disconnected suit can cause a bad frostbite at 30,000 feet. It is dreadfully cold up there.

It is daylight now and a cold wind is blowing. The men go back to the armament room and pick up their guns. A truck is waiting for them. They stow the guns carefully on the floor and then stiffly hoist themselves in. The truck drives away along the deserted runway. It moves into a side runway. Now you can see the ships set here and there on the field. A little group of men is collected under the wings of each one.

"There she is," the ball-turret man says. "I wonder if they got her nose repaired." It was the *Mary Ruth* that got her nose smashed by cartridge cases from a ship ahead. The truck draws up right under the nose of the great ship. The crew piles out and each man lifts his gun down tenderly. They go into the ship. The guns must be mounted and carefully tested. Ammunition must be checked and the guns loaded. It all takes time. That's why the men were awakened so long before the take-off time. A thousand things must be set before the take-off.

*　　　*

THE GROUND CREW

BOMBER STATION IN ENGLAND, *July 2, 1943*—The ground crew is still working over the *Mary Ruth*. Master Sergeant Pierce, of Oregon, is the crew chief. He has been long in the Army and he knows his engines. They say of him that he owns the *Mary Ruth* but he lends her to the skipper occasionally. If he says a flight is off, it is off. He has been checking the engines a good part of the night.

Corporal Harold is there, too. He has been loading bombs and seeing that the armament of the ship is in condition. The ground crew scurry about like rabbits. Their time is getting short. They have the obscure job, the job without glory and without publicity, and the ships could not fly without them. They are dressed in coveralls and baseball caps.

The gunners have mounted their guns by now and are testing the slides. A ground man is polishing the newly mended nose, rubbing every bit of dirt from it, so that the bombardier may have a good sight of his target.

A jeep drives up, carrying the officers—Brown, Quenin, Bliley, and Feerick. They spill a number of little square packets on the ground, one for each man. Captain Brown distributes them. They contain money of the countries near the target, concentrated food, and maps. Brown says, "Now, if we should get into any trouble don't go in the direction of ——— because the people haven't been very friendly there. Go toward ——— you'll find plenty of help there." The men take the packets and slip them in pockets below the knees in their coveralls.

The sun is just below the horizon now and there are fine pink puff clouds all over the sky. The captain looks at his watch. I guess we better get going," he says. The other Brown, the tail gunner, runs over. He hands over two rings, a cameo and another. "I forgot to leave these," he says. "Will you put them under my pillow?" The crew scramble to their places and the door is slammed and locked. The waist doors are open, of course, with the guns peering out of them, lashed down now, but immediately available. The long scallop of the cartridge belts drapes into each one.

The captain waves from his high perch. His window sits right over the ship's name—*Mary Ruth, Memories of Mobile*. The engines turn over and catch one at a time and roar as they warm up. And now, from all over the field, come the bursting roars of starting engines. From all over the field the great ships come rumbling from their dispersal points into the main runways. They make a line like giant bugs, a parade of them, moving down to the take-off stretch.

The captain signals and two ground-crew men dart in and pull out the chocks from in front of the wheels and dart out again. The *Mary Ruth* guns her motors and then slowly crawls out along her entrance and joins the parade. Along the runway the first ship whips out and gathers speed and takes the air, and behind her comes another and behind another and behind another, until the flying line of ships stretches away to the north. For a little while the squadron has disappeared, but in a few minutes back they come over the field, but this time they are not in a line. They have gained altitude and are flying in a tight formation. They go roaring over the field and they have hardly passed when another squadron from another field comes over, and then another and another. They will rendezvous at a given point, the squadrons from many fields, and when the whole force has gathered there will be perhaps a hundred of the great ships flying in Vs and in Vs of Vs, each protecting itself and the others by its position. And this great flight is going south like geese in the fall.

There is incredible detail to get these missions off. Staff detail of supply and intelligence detail, deciding and briefing the targets, and personnel detail of assigning the crews, and mechanical detail of keeping the engines going. *Bomb Boogie* went out with the others, but in a little while she flutters back with a dead motor. She has conked out again. No one can know why. She sinks dispiritedly to the ground.

When the mission has gone the ground crews stand about looking lonesome. They have watched every bit of the take-off and now they are left to sweat out the day until the ships come home. It is hard to set down the relation of the ground crew to the air crew, but there is something very close between them. This ground crew will be nervous and anxious until the ships come home. And if the *Mary Ruth* should fail to return they will go into a kind of sullen, wordless mourning. They have been working all night. Now they pile on a tractor to ride back to the hangar to get a cup of coffee in the mess hall. Master Sergeant Pierce says, "That's a good ship. Never did have any trouble with her. She'll come back, unless she's shot to pieces." In the barracks it is very quiet; the beds are unmade, their blankets hanging over the sides of the iron bunks. The pin-up girls look a little haggard in their sequin gowns. The family pictures are on the tops of the steel lockers. A clock ticking sounds strident. The rings go under Brown's pillow.

*   *

WAITING

BOMBER STATION IN ENGLAND, *July 4, 1943*—The field is deserted after the ships have left. The ground crew go into barracks to get some sleep, because they have been working most of the night. The flag hangs limply over the administration building. In the hangars repair crews are working over ships that have been injured. *Bomb Boogie* is brought in to be given another overhaul and *Bomb Boogie's* crew goes disgustedly back to bed.

The crews own a number of small dogs. These dogs, most of which are of uncertain or, at least, of ambiguous breed, belong to no one man. The ship usually owns each one, and the crew is very proud of him. Now these dogs wander disconsolately about the field. The life has gone out of the bomber station. The morning passes slowly. The squadron was due over the target at 9:52. It was due home at 12:43. As 9:50 comes and passes you have the ships in your mind. Now the flak has come up at them. Perhaps now a swarm of fighters has hurled itself at them. The thing happens in your mind. Now, if everything has gone well and there have been no accidents, the bomb bays are open and the ships are running over the target. Now they have turned and are making the run for home, keeping the formation tight, climbing, climbing to avoid the flak. It is 10 o'clock, they should be started back—10:20, they should be seeing the ocean by now.

The crew last night had told a story of the death of a Fortress, and it comes back to mind.

It was a beautiful day, they said, a picture day with big clouds and a very blue sky. The kind of day you see in advertisements for air travel back at home. The formation was flying toward St. Nazaire and the air was very clear. They could see the little towns on the ground, they said. Then the flak came up, they said, and some Messerschmitts parked off out of range and began to pot at them with their cannon. They didn't see where the Fortress up ahead was hit. Probably in the controls, because they did not see her break up at all.

They all agree that what happened seemed to happen very slowly. The Fortress slowly nosed up and up until she tried to climb vertically and, of course, she couldn't do that. Then she slipped in slow motion, backing like a falling leaf, and she balanced for a while and then her nose edged over and she started, nose down, for the ground.

The blue sky and the white clouds made a picture of it. The crew could see the gunner trying to get out and then he did, and his parachute fluffed open. And the ball-turret gunner— they could see him flopping about. The bombardier and navigator blossomed out of the nose and the waist gunners followed them. *Mary Ruth's* crew was yelling, "Get out, you pilots." The ship was far down when the ball-turret gunner cleared. They thought the skipper and the co-pilot were lost. They stayed with the ship too long and then—the ship was so far down that they could hardly see it. It must have been almost to the ground when two little puffs of white, first one and then the second, shot out of her. And the crew yelled with relief. And then the ship hit the ground and exploded. Only the tail gunner and ball-turret man had seen the end. They explained it over the intercom.

Beside the no. 1 hangar there is a little mound of earth covered with short, heavy grass. At 12:15 the ground men begin to congregate on it and sweat out the homecoming. Rumor comes with the crew chief that they have reported, but it is rumor. A small dog, which might be a gray Scottie if his ears didn't hang down and his tail bend the wrong way, comes to sit on the little mound. He stretches out and puts his whiskery muzzle on his outstretched paws. He does not close his eyes and his ears twitch. All the ground crews are there now, waiting for their ships. It is the longest set of minutes imaginable.

Suddenly the little dog raises his head. His body begins to tremble all over. The crew chief has a pair of field glasses. He looks down at the dog and then aims his glasses to the south. "Can't see anything yet," he says. The little dog continues to shudder and a high whine comes from him.

And here they come. You can just see the dots far to the south. The formation is good, but one ship flies alone and ahead. "Can you see her number? Who is she?" The lead ship drops altitude and comes in straight for the field. From her side two little rockets break, a red one and a white one. The ambulance, they call it the meat wagon, starts down the runway. There is a hurt man on that ship.

The main formation comes over the field and each ship peels to circle for a landing, but the lone ship drops and the wheels strike the ground and the Fortress lands like a great bug on the runway. But the moment her wheels are on the ground there is a sharp, crying bark and a streak of gray. The little dog seems hardly to touch the ground. He streaks across the field toward the landed ship. He knows his own ship. One by one the Fortresses land and the ground crews check off the numbers as they land. *Mary Ruth* is there. Only one ship is missing and she landed farther south, with short fuel tanks. There is a great sigh of relief on the mound. The mission is over.

*   *

DAY OF MEMORIES

LONDON, *July 4, 1943*—All the day there have been exercises and entertainments for the troops on leave in London. Everything that can be done for a guest has been done. There was a hay ride this morning. There have been exercises and dances and speeches, excursions to points of interest. The British and the Canadians and the others have been extra friendly. The bands in the parks played "The Star-Spangled Banner" and "Dixie" and "Home, Sweet Home." Everything has been done that can be done and this is a city of the most abject homesickness.

The speaker said in clipped and concise English, "We welcome you again on this day that is dear to you." And the minds were on the red-necked politician, foaming with enthusiasm and bourbon whisky, screaming the eagle on a bunting-covered platform while his audience longed for the watermelon and potato salad to come.

The conductors of parties said, "We are going to the Tower

of London. It is in a sense the cradle of English civilization"
—the fat man's race, the three-legged race, the squeals of
women running with eggs in tablespoons, the smell of barbecu-
ing meat on a deep pit.

The band played beautifully in Trafalgar Square a digni-
fied and compelling march—and Coney Island, in its welter of
squalling children, the smell of ice cream and peanuts and
water-soaked cigar butts, the surf, one-third water and two-
thirds people, fighting their way through the grapefruit rinds,
the squeak and bellow of honky-tonk music.

Soldiers have paraded in London, men who marched like
clothed machines, towering men, straight as their own rifles
and their hands swinging—at home, the knights of this and
that in wilted ostrich-plumed hats, in uniforms out of the moth-
balls again, knights who were butchers last evening, and clerks
and tellers of the local bank, but knights now, out of step,
shambling after their great banner, their tinsel swords at all
angles over their shoulders, the knights of this and that.

The hospitable people of London have served flan and trifles, biscuits and tea, marmalade, gin and lime, scotch and
water, and beer—hot dogs, with mustard drooling from the
lower end and running up your sleeve. Hamburgers, with raw
onions spilling out of the round buns. Popcorn dripping with
butter. The sting of neat whisky and the barrels of beer set
on trestles. Chocolate cakes and deviled eggs, but mostly hamburgers with onions, and which will have you have, piccalilli
or dill or mayonnaise, or all of them?

The cool girls dance well and they are pleasant and friendly.
They work hard in the war plants, and it's a job to get a dress
so neatly pressed. The lipstick is hard to get, and the perfume
is the last in the bottle. Neat and pretty and friendly. At home

the sticky kisses in the rumble seat and the swatting at mosquitoes on a hot, vine-covered porch. And in the joints the juke box howls and its basses thump the air. When you say something the girl knows the proper answer. None of it means anything, but it all fits together. Everything fits together.

This is a time of homesickness, and Christmas will be worse. No grandeur, no luxury, no interest can cut it out. No show is as good as the double bill at the Odeon, no food is as good as the midnight sandwich at Joe's, and no one in the world is as pretty as that blond Margie who works at the Poppy.

When they come home they'll be a little tiresome about London for a long time. They will recall exotic adventures and strange foods. Piccadilly and the Savoy and the White Tower, the Normandie Bar and the place in Soho will drip from their conversation. They will compare notes enthusiastically with other soldiers who were here. The cool girls will grow to strange and romantic adventures. The lonesome little glow will be remembered as a Bacchic orgy. They will remember things they did not know that they saw— St. Paul's against a lead-colored sky and the barrage balloons hanging over it. Waterloo Station, the sandbags piled high against the Wren churches, the excited siren and the sneak air raid.

But today, July 4, 1943, they wander about in a daze of homesickness, seeing nothing, hearing nothing but the faces and voices of their own people.

*   *

THE PEOPLE OF DOVER

DOVER, *July 6, 1943*—Dover, with its castle on the hill and its little crooked streets, its big, ugly hotels and its secret and dangerous offensive power, is closest of all to the enemy. Dover is full of the memory of Wellington and of Napoleon, of the time when Napoleon came down to Calais and looked across the Channel at England and knew that only this little stretch of water interrupted his conquest of the world. And later the men of Dunkerque dragged their weary feet off the little ships and struggled through the streets of Dover.

Then Hitler came to the hill above Calais and looked across at the cliffs, and again only the little stretch of water stopped the conquest of the world. It is a very little piece of water. On the clear days you can see the hills about Calais, and with a glass you can see the clock tower of Calais. When the guns of Calais fire you can see the flash, while with the telescope you can see from the castle the guns themselves, and even tanks deploying on the beach.

Dover feels very close to the enemy. Three minutes in a fast airplane, three-quarters of an hour in a fast boat. Every day or so a plane comes whipping through and drops a bomb and takes a shot or so at the balloons that hang in the air above the town, and every few days Jerry trains his big guns on Dover and fires a few rounds of high explosive at the little old town. Then a building is hit and collapses and sometimes a few people are killed. It is a wanton, useless thing, serving no military, naval, or morale business. It is almost as though the Germans fretted about the little stretch of water that defeated them.

There is a quality in the people of Dover that may well be the key to the coming German disaster. They are incorrigibly, incorruptibly unimpressed. The German, with his uniform and his pageantry and his threats and plans, does not impress these people at all. The Dover man has taken perhaps a little more pounding than most, not in great blitzes, but in every-day bombing and shelling, and still he is not impressed.

Jerry is like the weather to him. He complains about it and then promptly goes about what he was doing. Nothing in the world is as important as his garden and, in other days, his lobster pots. Weather and Jerry are alike in that they are inconvenient and sometimes make messes. Surveying a building wrecked by a big shell, he says, "Jerry was bad last night," as he would discuss a windstorm.

It goes like this—on the Calais hill there is a flash in the night. Immediately from Dover the sirens give the shelling warning. From the flash you must count approximately fifty-nine seconds before the explosion. The shell may land almost anywhere. There is a flat blast that rockets back from the cliffs, a cloud of debris rising into the air. People look at their watches. The next one will be in twenty minutes. And at exactly that time there is another flash from the French coast, and you count seconds again. This goes on sometimes all night. One hour after the last shell the all-clear sounds. This does not mean that it is over. Jerry sometimes lobs another one in, hoping to kill a few more people.

In the morning there are wrecked houses; the dead have been dug out. A little band of men are cleaning the debris out of the street so that traffic may go by. A policeman keeps the people from coming too close for fear a brick may fall. That house is probably wrecked and will be unlivable until the war is over, but the houses all about are hurt. The windows are all blown out, and there will be no glass until after the war, either. The people are already sticking paper over the broken windows. Plaster has fallen in the houses all about. A general house cleaning is in progress. Puffs of swept plaster come out the doors. Women are on their knees, with pails of water, washing the floors. The blast of a near shell cleans the chimneys, they say. The puff of the explosion blows the soot out of the chimney and into the rooms.

There is that to clean up, too. In a front yard a man is standing in his garden. A flying piece of scantling has broken off a rose bush. The bud, which was about to open, is wilting on the ground. The man leans down and picks up the bud. He feels it with his fingers and carries it to his nose and smells it. He lifts the scantling from the trunk and looks at it to see whether it may not send out new shoots, and then, standing up, he turns and looks at the French coast, where five hundred men and a great tube of steel and high explosive and charts and plans, mathematical formulae, uniforms, telephones, shouted orders, are out to break a man's rose bush. A neighbor passes in the street.

"The Boche was bloody bad last night," he says. "Broke the yellow one proper," he says. "And it was just coming on to bloom."

"Ah, well," the neighbor says, "let's have a look at it." The two kneel down beside the bush. "She's broke above the graft," the neighbor says, "she's not split. Probably shoot out here." He points with a thick finger to a lump on the side of the bush. "Sometimes," he says, "sometimes, when they've had a shock, they come out prettier than ever."

Across the Channel, in back of the hill that you can see, they are cleaning the great barrel, studying charts, making reports, churning with Geopolitik.

*   *

MINESWEEPER

LONDON, *July 7, 1943*—Day after day the mine-sweepers go out. Small boats that in peacetime fished for her-ring and cod. Now they fish for bigger game. They are equipped with strange, new fish lines. The crews are nearly all ex-fishermen and whalers and the officers are from the same tough breed. Theirs is an unromantic and unpublicized job that must be done and done very thoroughly. The danger lurks without flags and firing. Very few decorations are awarded to the minesweeping men.

They usually sail out of the harbor in a line, three boats to sweep and two to drop the buoyed flags, called dans, which mark the swept channel. Once on the ground to be swept, three of the boats deploy and travel abreast at exact and set distances from one another. The space between them is the area that can be reached by their instruments. The little boats are searching for the two kinds of mines which are usually planted—the magnetic mines which explode when a ship with its self-created magnetic field sails over, and the other kind which is exploded by the vibration of a ship's engines. The sweepers are equipped with instruments to explode either kind and to do it at a safe distance from themselves.

The three abreast move slowly over the area to be cleared of mines and behind them the dan ships follow at intervals, putting out the flags. At the end of their run they turn and come back, overlapping a little on the old course and the dan ships pick up the flags and set them on the outer course again.

All the boats are armed against airplanes. The gunners stand at their posts and search the sky constantly, while the radio operator listens to the spotting instruments on the shore. They take no chances with the planes. When one comes near them they train their guns in that direction until they recognize her. And even the friendly planes do not fly too close. For these men have been bombed and fired on from the air so often that they will fire if there is any doubt at all. Sticking up out of the water are the masts of many ships sunk early in the war when the German planes ranged over the Channel almost with impunity. They do not do it any more.

The voice of the radio man comes up through the speaking tube to the little bridge. "Enemy aircraft in the vicinity," he says, and then a moment later, "Red alert." The gunners swing their guns and the crew stands by, all eyes on the sky. From the English coast the Typhoons boil out angrily, fast and deadly ships that fly close to the water. In the distance the enemy plane is a spot. It turns tail and runs for the French coast. The radio man calls, "All clear," and the crew relaxes.

On the little bridge the captain directs the laying down of the colored flags, while his second checks the distance between the boats. If the dan ship gets too close, a mine may explode under her. With instruments the distance is checked every few seconds. The little flotilla moves very slowly, for when it has passed and marked the free channel the ships with supplies must be able to come through in safety.

Suddenly the dan ship is struck by a heavy blow, the sea about flattens out and shivers, and then a hundred yards ahead a tower of water and mud bursts into the air with a roar. It seems to hang in the air for a long time and when it falls back the dan ship is nearly over it.

There is a large, dirty place on the ocean, bottom mud and a black gluey substance, which comes from the explosive. The crew rush to the side of the ship and search the water anxiously. "No fish," they say. "What has happened to the fish? You'd think there would be one or two killed by the blast." They have set off one of the most terrible weapons in the world and they are worried about the fish.

The captain marks with great care on his chart the exact

place where the mine was exploded. He takes several sights on the coast to get the position. Another mine roars up on the other side of the lane. The second in command takes up the blinker and signals, "Any fish?" and the answer comes back, "No fish."

The day is long and tedious, sweeping and turning and sweeping, and when the job is done it is only done until the night, for on this night the mine layers may creep over from the French coast and sow the field again with the nasty things, or a plane may fly low in the darkness and drop the mines on parachutes. The work of the sweepers is never finished.

It is late when they turn for home and it is dark when the little ships file into the harbor and tie up to the pier. Then the captain and his second relax. The strain goes out of their faces. No matter how long or uneventful the sweep, the danger is never gone. The gun crew clean and cover their guns and go to their quarters. The officers climb down to the tiny wardroom. They kick off their fleece-lined boots and settle back into their chairs. The captain picks up the work he has been doing for weeks. He is making a beautifully exact model of—a minesweeper.

*   *

COAST BATTERY

SOMEWHERE IN ENGLAND, *July 8, 1943*—The guns hide in a field of grain and red poppies. You can see the cannon muzzles protruding and aiming at the sky. The battery is on the south coast, in sight of France. There was a time when great flights of German bombers came over this undefended coast and carried their bomb loads to London and Canterbury. But the coast is not undefended now.

The spotters are all over the hills, the complicated and delicate listening posts which can hear a plane miles away, and the spotters are girls. When a strange ship is heard, its position is phoned to the plotters of position, and the plotters are girls, too. The sighters are girls. Only the gunners who load and turn the gun itself are men. It is an amazing institution, the mixed battery, something unique in the history of armies.

The barracks are nearby, one for the girls and another for the men. The eating hall is common, the recreation room is common, and the work is common.

Twenty-four hours a day the crews are on duty. They can do what they want within a certain distance from the gun. The girls read and wash their clothing, sew and cook. The kitchen, a temporary affair, is built of kerosene tins filled with sand laid like bricks. The new kitchen is just now being built.

The countryside is quiet. The guns are silent. Suddenly the siren howls. Buildings that are hidden in camouflage belch people, young men and women. They pour out, running like mad. The siren has not been going for thirty seconds when the run is over, the gun is manned, the target spotted. In the control room under ground the instruments have found their target. A girl has fixed it. The numbers have been transmitted and the ugly barrels whirled. Above ground, in a concrete box, a girl speaks into a telephone. "Fire," she says quietly. The hillside rocks with the explosion of the battery. The field grass shakes and the red poppies shudder in the blast. New orders come up from below and the girl says, "Fire."

The process is machine-like, exact. There is no waste movement and no nonsense. These girls seem to be natural soldiers. They *are* soldiers, too. They resent above anything being treated like women when they are near the guns. Their work is hard and constant. Sometimes they are alerted to the guns thirty times in a day and a night. They may fire on a marauder ten times in that period. They have been bombed and strafed, and there is no record of any girl flinching.

The commander is very proud of them. He is fiercely affectionate toward his battery. He says a little bitterly, "All right, why don't you ask about the problem of morals? Everyone wants to know about that. I'll tell you—there is no problem."

He tells about the customs that have come into being in this battery, a set of customs which grew automatically. The men and the women sing together, dance together, and, let any one of the women be insulted, and he has the whole battery on his neck. But when a girl walks out in the evening, it is not with one of the battery men, nor do the men take the girls to the movies. There have been no engagements and no marriages between members of the battery. Some instinct among the people themselves has told them trouble would result. These things are not a matter of orders but of custom.

The girls like this work and are proud of it. It is difficult to see how the housemaids will be able to go back to dusting furniture under querulous mistresses, how the farm girls will be able to go back to the tiny farms of Scotland and the Midlands. This is the great exciting time of their lives. They are very important, these girls. The defense of the country in their area is in their hands.

The manager of the local theater has set aside two rows of seats this evening for members of the battery who are off duty. The girls who are to go change from their trousers to neat khaki skirts and blouses. They spend a good deal of time making themselves pretty. They sit in the theater, leaning forward with excitement. The film is a little stinker called *War Correspondent*, made six thousand miles from any conflict, where people are not likely ever to see any.

It concerns an American war correspondent who through pure handsomeness, cleverness, bravery, and hokum defeats every resource of the Third Reich. The Gestapo and the German Army are putty in his hands. It is a veritable Flynn of a picture.

And these girls who have been bombed and strafed, who have shot enemies out of the sky and then gone back to mending socks—are these girls scornful? Not in the least. They sit on the edges of their seats. When the stupid Gestapo men creep up to the hero they shriek to warn him. This is more real to them than this afternoon, when they fired on a Focke Wulf 190. The hero who emerges from a one-man Dunkerque, with combed hair and immaculate dress, is the true, the good, the beautiful.

This afternoon the girls were sweaty, dusty, and they smelled of cordite. That was their job—this is war. And when the film is done they walk back to their barracks, talking excitedly of the glories of Hollywood warfare. They go back to their routine job of defending the coast of England from attack, and as they walk home they sing, "You'd be sooo naice to come 'ome to, You'd be so naice by a fire."

*   *

ALCOHOLIC GOAT

LONDON, *July 9, 1943*—His name is Wing Commander William Goat, DSO, and he is old and honored, and, some say, in iniquity. But when he joined the RAF wing two years ago he was just able to totter about on long and knobby legs. For a long time he was treated like any other recruit—kicked about, ignored, and at times cursed. But gradually his abilities began to be apparent. He is very good luck to have about. When he is near, his wing has good fortune and good hunting. Gradually his horns, along with his talents, developed, until now his rank and his decorations are painted on his horns in brilliant colors and he carries himself with a shambling strut.

He will eat nearly everything. No party nor any review is complete without him. At one party, being left alone for a few moments, it is reported that he ate two hundred sandwiches, three cakes, the arrangements for piano and flute of "Pomp and Circumstance," drank half a bowl of punch, and then walked jauntily among the dancers, belching slightly and regarding a certain lieutenant's wife, who shall be nameless, with a lustful eye.

He has the slightly bilious look of the military of the higher brackets. Being an air-goat, he has rather unique habits. If you bring an oxygen bottle into view, he rushes to it and demands it. He puts his whole mouth over the outlet and then, as you turn the valve, he gently relaxes, grunting happily, and his sides fill out until he nearly bursts. Just before he bursts he lets go of the nozzle and collapses slowly, but the energy he takes from the oxygen makes him leap into the air and engage imaginary goats in horny combat. He also loves the glycol cooling fluid which is used in the engines of the Typhoons. For hours he will stand under the barrels, licking the drips from the spouts.

He has the confidence of his men. Once when it was required that his wing change its base of operations quickly, he was left behind, for in those days it was not known how important he was. At the new base the men were nervous and irritable, fearful and almost mutinous. Finally, when it was seen that they would not relax, a special plane had to be sent to pick up the wing commander and transport him to the new base. Once he arrived, everything settled down. The Typhoons had four kills within twenty-four hours. The nervous tension went out of the air, the food got better as the cook ceased brooding, and a number of stomach complaints disappeared immediately.

Wing Commander Goat lives in a small house behind the Operations Room. His name and honors are painted over the door. It is very good luck to go to him and stroke his sides and rub his horns before going out on operations. He does not go out on operations himself. There is not room in the Typhoons for him, but if it were possible to squeeze him in he would be taken, and then heaven knows what great action might not take place.

This goat has only one truly bad habit. He loves beer, and furthermore is able to absorb it in such quantities that even the mild, nearly non-alcoholic English beer can make him tipsy. In spite of orders to the contrary he is able to seek out the evil companions who will give him beer. Once inebriated, he is prone to wander about sneering. He sneers at the American Army Air Force, he sneers at the Labor party, and once he sneered at Mr. Churchill. The sneer is probably inherent in the beer, since punch has quite a different effect on him.

In appearance this goat is not impressive. He has a shabby, pinkish fur and a cold, fishlike eye; his legs are not straight, in fact he is slightly knockkneed. He carries his head high and his horns, painted in brilliant red and blue, more than offset any physical oddness. In every way, he is a military figure. He is magnificent on parade. Eventually he will be given a crypt in the Air Ministry and will die in good time of that military ailment, cirrhosis of the liver. He will be buried with full military honors.

But meanwhile Wing Commander William Goat, DSO, is the luck of his wing, and his loss would cause great unrest and even despondency.

*   *

STORIES OF THE BLITZ

LONDON, *July 10, 1943*—People who try to tell you what the blitz was like in London start with fire and explosion and then almost invariably end up with some very tiny detail which crept in and set and became the symbol of the whole thing for them. Again and again this happens in conversations. It is as though the mind could not take in the terror and the noise of the bombs and the general horror and so fastened on something small and comprehensible and ordinary. Everyone who was in London during the blitz wants to describe it, wants to solidify, if only for himself, something of that terrible time.

"It's the glass," says one man, "the sound in the morning of the broken glass being swept up, the vicious, flat tinkle. That is the thing I remember more than anything else, that constant sound of broken glass being swept up on the pavements. My dog broke a window the other day and my wife swept up the glass and a cold shiver went over me. It was a moment before I could trace the reason for it."

You are going to dine at a small restaurant. There is a ruin across the street from the place, a jagged, destroyed stone house. Your companion says, "On one of the nights I had an engagement to have dinner with a lady at this very place. She was to meet me here. I got here early and then a bomb hit that one." He points to the ruin. "I went out in the street. You could see plainly, the fires lighted the whole city. That front wall was spilled into the street. You could see the front of a cab sticking out from the pile of fallen stone. Thrown clear, right at my feet as I came out of the door, was one pale blue evening slipper. The toe of it was pointing right at me."

Another points up at a wall; the building is gone, but there are five fireplaces, one above another, straight up the wall. He points to the topmost fireplace. "This was a high-explosive bomb," he says. "This is on my way to work. You know, for six months there was a pair of long stockings hanging in front of that fireplace. They must have been pinned up. They hung there for months, just as they had been put up to dry."

"I was passing Hyde Park," says a man, "when a big raid came over. I went down into the gutter. Always did that when you couldn't get a shelter. I saw a great tree, one like those, jump into the air and fall on its side not so far from me —right there where that scoop is in the ground. And then a sparrow fell in the gutter right beside me. It was dead all right. Concussion kills birds easily. For some reason I picked it up and held it for a long time. There was no blood on it or anything like that. I took it home with me. Funny thing, I had to throw it right away."

One night, when the bombs screamed and blatted, a refugee who had been driven from place to place and tortured in all of them until he finally reached London, couldn't stand it any more. He cut his throat and jumped out of a high window. A girl, who was driving an ambulance that night, says, "I remember how angry I was with him. I understand it a little now, but that night I was furious with him. There were so many who got it that night and they couldn't help it. I shouted at him I hoped he would die, and he did.

"People save such strange things. One elderly man lost his whole house by fire. He saved an old rocking chair. He took it everywhere with him; wouldn't leave it for a moment. His whole family was killed, but he hung on to that rocking chair. He wouldn't sit in it. He sat on the ground beside it, but you couldn't get it away from him."

Two reporters sat out the blitz in the Savoy Hotel, playing chess and fortifying themselves. When the bombs came near they went under the table. "One or the other of us always reached up and cheated a little," the reporter says.

Hundreds of stories, and all of them end with a little incident, a little simple thing that stays in your mind.

"I remember the eyes of people going to work in the morning," a man says. "There was a quality of tiredness in those eyes I haven't forgotten. It was beyond a tiredness you can imagine—a desperate kind of weariness that never expected to be rested. The eyes of the people seemed to be deep, deep in their heads, and their voices seemed to come from a long distance. And I remember during a raid seeing a blind man standing on the curb, tapping with his stick and waiting for someone to take him across through the traffic. There wasn't any traffic, and the air was full of fire, but he stood there and tapped until someone came along and took him to a shelter."

In all of the little stories it is the ordinary, the common-place thing or incident against the background of the bombing that leaves the indelible picture.

"An old woman was selling little miserable sprays of sweet lavender. The city was rocking under the bombs and the light of burning buildings made it like day. The air was just one big fat blasting roar. And in one little hole in the roar her voice got in—a squeaky voice. 'Lavender!' she said. 'Buy Lavender for luck.' "

The bombing itself grows vague and dreamlike. The little pictures remain as sharp as they were when they were new.

*   *

LILLI MARLENE

LONDON, *July 12, 1943*—This is the story of a song. Its name is "Lilli Marlene" and it was written in Germany in 1938 by Norbert Schultze and Hans Leit. In due course they tried to publish it and it was rejected by about two dozen publishers. Finally it was taken up by a singer, Lala Anderson, a Swedish girl, who used it for her signature song. Lala

Anderson has a husky voice and is what you might call the Hildegarde type.

"Lilli Marlene" is a very simple song. The first verse of it goes: "Underneath the lanterns, by the barracks square, I used to meet Marlene and she was young and fair." The song was as simple as that. It went on to tell about Marlene, who first liked stripes and then shoulder bars. Marlene met more and more people until, finally, she met a brigadier, which was what she wanted all along. We have a song with much the same amused cynicism.

Eventually Lala made a record of the song and even it was not very popular. But one night the German station in Belgrade, which sent out programs to Rommel's Afrika Korps, found that, due to a little bombing, it did not have many records left, but among a few uninjured disks was the song "Lilli Marlene." It was put on the air to Africa and by the next morning it was being hummed by the Afrika Korps and letters were going in demanding that it be played again.

The story of its popularity in Africa got back to Berlin, and Madame Goering, who used to be an opera singer, sang the song of the inconstant "Lilli Marlene" to a very select group of Nazis, if there is such a thing. Instantly the song was popular and it was played constantly over the German radio until Goering himself grew a little sick of it, and it is said that, since inconstancy is a subject which is not pleasant to certain high Nazi ears, it was suggested that the song be quietly assassinated. But meanwhile "Lilli Marlene" had got out of hand. Lala Anderson was by now known as the "Soldiers' Sweetheart." She was a pin-up girl. Her husky voice ground out of portable phonographs in the desert.

So far, "Lilli" had been solely a German problem, but now

the British Eighth Army began to take prisoners and among the spoils they got "Lilli Marlene." And the song swept through the Eighth Army. Australians hummed it and fastened new words to it. The powers hesitated, considering whether it was a good idea to let a German song about a girl who did not have all the sterling virtues become the favorite song of the British Army, for by now the thing had crept into the First Army and the Americans were beginning to experiment with close harmony and were putting an off-beat into it. It wouldn't have done the powers a bit of good if they had decided against the song.

It was out of hand. The Eighth Army was doing all right in the field and it was decided to consider "Lilli Marlene" a prisoner of war, which would have happened anyway, no matter what the powers thought about it. Now "Lilli" is getting deeply into the American Forces in Africa. The Office of War Information took up the problem and decided to keep the melody, but to turn new words against the Germans. Whether this will work or not remains to be seen. "Lilli Marlene" is international. It is to be suspected that she will emerge beside the barrack walls—young and fair and incorruptly inconsistent.

There is nothing you can do about a song like this except to let it go. War songs need not be about the war at all. Indeed, they rarely are. In the last war, "Madelon" and "Tipperary" had nothing to do with war. The great Australian song of this war, "Waltzing Matilda," concerns itself with sheep-stealing. It is to be expected that some groups in America will attack "Lilli," first, on the ground that she is an enemy alien, and, second, because she is no better than she should be. Such attacks will have little effect. "Lilli" is immortal. Her simple desire to meet a brigadier is hardly a German copyright. Politics may be dominated and nationalized, but songs have a way of leaping boundaries.

And it would be amusing if, after all the fuss and heiling, all the marching and indoctrination, the only contribution to the world by the Nazis was "Lilli Marlene."

*   *

WAR TALK

LONDON, *July 13, 1943*—It is interesting to see that the nearer one comes to a war zone the less one hears of grand strategy. There is more discussion of tactics and the over-all picture in the Stork Club on a Saturday night than in the whole European theater of operations. This may be, to a certain extent, because of a lack of generals to give the strategists a social foundation. For that matter, there are more generals in the Carlton Hotel in Washington at lunch time than in all the rest of the world.

This narrowing point of view may be geographical. Papers in England are not avidly seized, and as one gets down to the coast where some action is going on all the time, the discussion of the war dwindles until it almost disappears. It is further interesting how completely civilian ferocity disappears from the soldier or the sailor close to action or in action.

In the concrete wardroom over the berths of the motor torpedo boats the young men gather to drink beer. They are very young men, but there is an age in their faces that comes of having put their lives out at stake too often. The dice have rolled right for some of these young men so far, but a seven has turned up for too many of their friends for them to take the game or their luck for granted. The little boats are not heavily armed for defense, but they carry terrible blows in their torpedo tubes. They are the only lightweights in the world that can deliver a heavyweight punch. For their own safety they have only their speed and the cleverness of their crews.

Tonight they are going out on what the men call a Thing. A Thing is something bigger than a Scramble, but slightly less large than The Thing. A Thing is likely to be an attack on a German convoy, slipping secretly in the night through the Channel, but heavily armed and heavily guarded and, moreover, hugging the coast so that they are under the shore guns most of the time. And against them these tiny ships are going to dodge in under the shellfire, twist and turn in the paths of the tracers, and, finally, shoot their torpedoes into the largest ship they can find and then race for home.

In the wardroom the men speak with a kind of intense gaiety. You never hear the enemy discussed. By unstated agreement or because there has just been too much war they do not discuss war. The enemy is Jerry, or the Boche, and his name is spoken as something disembodied and vague. Jerry is a problem in navigation, a job, a danger, but not much more personalized than any other big and dangerous job. The men suffer from strain. It has been so long applied that they are probably not even conscious of it. It isn't fear, but it is something you can feel, a bubble that grows bigger and bigger in your mid-section. It puffs up against your lungs so that your breathing becomes short. Sitting around is bad. You have a tendency to think that everything is very funny. This is the time to bring out the frowsy story that wouldn't do so well at any other time. It will get a roar of laughter now.

There is a little bar in the wardroom where a Wren serves the flat beer that no one likes. The beer isn't good, but everyone has a glass of it, and it is hard to swallow, because so much of you is taken up with the big bubble.

On the wall there is a clock and the hands creep slowly, much too slowly, toward the operation time. The waiting is the terrible part. The weather reports come in. There is wind, but perhaps not enough to cancel the Thing. Dozens of the little ships are going out. It is an Allied operation. There are Dutch boats, and Polish boats, and English. The Poles are great fighters. This is their kind of work. When the little ships attacked the *Scharnhorst,* slipping through the Channel, it is said that a Polish sailor was down on the prow of his torpedo boat, calmly firing at the great steel battleship with a rifle. The Dutch have a calm, cold courage, and the British pretend, as usual, it is some kind of a garden party they are going to.

At ten minutes to the time the men start to get into their suits, complicated coats and trousers of oilskin that tie closely around the ankles. A towel is wrapped around the neck and the coat buttoned in tight about it. The little ships are wet. The green water comes over the bow constantly and there isn't much cover. In action the men will presumably wear helmets on their heads, but this is only a presumption. Now they stand about, padded and wadded, their arms a little out from their sides, held out by the thick clothing. The leader of this group is a young man of great age. He is twenty-two and he came from a destroyer to the little MTBs. The big hand of the clock creeps on to the time of departure. The commander says, almost casually, and just as it is on the minute, "All ready?"

All the young men stride heavily out of the door, down the steps to the hidden pens where the little stinging fish lie. There is a roar as engine after engine starts. Now the bubble bursts in your stomach and you can breathe again. Everything is all right. It's a good night, misty and with little visibility. The boats back, one by one, from their berths and fall into line. A tiny blinker signals from the leader, the great motors thunder, the boats leap forward, and the white wake Vs out. The green water comes in over the bow. The crew huddles down, braced against the wind and the sea—no one has mentioned the war.

*   *

THE COTTAGE THAT WASN'T THERE

LONDON, *July 14, 1943*—The sergeant lay in the grass and pulled grass and bit off the tender stems and chewed them. It was Sunday, and a number of people were lying about, sailors and soldiers and even a few civilians. Across the path a line of people were fishing in the Serpentine, sitting on rented chairs, fishing in water that was stirred with the oars of boats and kicking swans. Each fisherman had his little audience.

The sergeant said, "This is a crazy country. Look at that, there hasn't been a fish caught there all day, and they go right on with it. Maybe they're not after fish. It's a crazy country, and it's getting me nuts, too." He spat out a little chewed wad of green grass stems. "I've got something bothering me," he said. "It's a ghost story. I don't believe it happened, and I know it happened. Only I don't believe in ghosts. I've been thinking about it, sniffing around it, and I can't make any sense out of it.

"You see," he said, "I'm at a little station up in the country. Not a very big outfit. There is a village about a mile from camp, and in the evening we walk in and get a couple of glasses of beer and try to figure out this darts game."

Far up the line of fishermen a man caught a fish about the size of a sardine and caused so much excitement that he was surrounded by people in a moment. The sergeant chuckled. "I used to work salmon in the Columbia River," he said, and let it go at that. "Well, anyway," he said, "it came on toward dark, and I've got some paper work to do, so I figured I'd walk back to camp. The other fellows weren't ready to go yet. They're kidding the barmaid, telling her they know movie stars. So I started out alone.

"I've been over that little road at least a hundred times. I know every foot of it, I guess. It's a narrow, little road, with hedges on both sides, so you can't see into the fields. The road is kind of cut down, like a trench. It's not a very dark night, at least there is some starlight, and you can see big clouds, like it was going to rain." He stopped and seemed to be considering whether he should go on at all. He was looking

69

across the Serpentine at the little pavilion where they rent boats, where the line of people wait all day for their turn to rent a boat.

The sergeant made up his mind suddenly. "About halfway back there was a light out onto the road. There was a little cottage, kind of, with the hedge coming up to it on both sides. There is a garden in front, a fence and then this big square window with little panes. Well, the light is coming out of that window. I looked right through and could see the room. It was kind of pleasant. There was a lamp on the table, and a fire in a small fireplace. It was kind of pleasant. It wasn't a very bright light, but you could see pretty well. There's a white cat asleep on the seat of a chair, and sitting beside the table under the lamp is a woman about fifty, I should say, and she is sewing on something. I stood there. Peeping-Tommed for a couple of minutes. It was peaceful and cozy-looking and nice.

"In a minute I walked on. There was something bothering me in the back of my mind. And then I thought, 'Sure that's what it is, no blackout curtains.' I hadn't seen a light coming out of the window at night for ten months—that's how long I've been over. I was going to go back and tell that woman to pull her blackout curtains in case some country cop came along. She'd get a stiff fine. I turned around and looked back. I couldn't see the cottage, but I could see the light shining out in the road. Well then, I thought, 'What the hell, maybe no cop will come by.' It looked so nice, the room and the fire that you could look in on. You get awful tired of the black-out."

The sergeant picked up a little twig, dug at a grass root with it. "I walked along, but there was something that kept ticking away in my head, something I couldn't get hold of. It began to sprinkle a little bit of rain, but not enough to hurt anything. I thought about the work I had to do, but I couldn't get away from the feeling that there was something wrong with something."

He dug out his grass root, and it came up with a little lump of soil in it. He shook the dirt out of it. "I was just about to turn into the camp when it plumped into my mind. Now, this is what it is. And I've been thinking about it, and I can't figure it out. There isn't any cottage there, just four stone walls all black with fire. Early in the blitz some Jerry dropped a fire bomb on that cottage."

His fingers were restless. They were trying to plant the grass roots again in the hole they had come out of. "You see what worries me about the whole thing is this," he said. "I just don't believe stuff like that."

*   *

GROWING VEGETABLES

LONDON, *July 15, 1943*—On the edges of American airfields and between the barracks of troops in England it is no unusual thing to see complicated and carefully tended vegetable gardens. No one seems to know where the idea originated, but these gardens have been constantly increasing. It is fairly common now that a station furnishes a good part of its own vegetables and all of its own salad greens.

The idea, which had as its basis, probably, the taking up of some of the free time of men where there were few entertainment facilities, has proved vastly successful. The gardens are run by the units and worked by the groups, but here and there a man may go out on his own and try and raise some strange seed which is not ordinarily seen in this climate. In every unit there is usually some man who knows about such things who advises on the planting, but even such men are often at a loss because vegetables are different here from the vegetables at home.

The things that the men want to raise most, in order of choice, are green corn, tomatoes, and peppers. None of these do very well in England unless there is a glass house to build up sufficient heat. Tomatoes are small; there are none of those master beefsteak tomatoes bursting with juice. It is a short, cool season. Green corn has little chance to mature and the peppers must be raised under glass. Nevertheless, every care is taken to raise them. Men who are homesick seem to take a mighty pleasure in working with the soil.

The gardens usually start out ambitiously. Watermelons and cantaloupes are planted and they have practically no chance of maturing at this latitude, where even cucumbers are usually raised in glass houses, but gradually some order grows out of the confusion. Lettuce, peas, green beans, green onions, potatoes do very well here, as do cabbages and turnips and beets and carrots. The gardens are lush and well tended. In the evenings, which are very long now, the men work in the beds. It does not get dark until eleven o'clock, there are only so many movies to be seen, English pubs are not exciting, but there does seem to be a constant excitement about the gardens, and the produce that comes from them tastes much better than that purchased in the open market.

One station has its headquarters in a large English country house which at one time must have been very luxurious. Part of the equipment of this place is a series of glass houses, and here the gardens are exceptional. There has never been any need to exert pressure to get the men to work in the gardens. They have taken it up with enthusiasm and in many cases men from the cities, who have never had a garden in their lives, have become enthusiastic. There is some contact with the normal about the garden, a kind of relationship with peace.

Now and then a garden just coming in to produce must be deserted as the unit is shifted to another area. But this does not seem to make any difference. The new unit takes over the garden, and the old one, if there is none at the new station, starts afresh. The value is in the doing of it. The morale value of the experiment is very high, so high that it is being suggested that supply officers should be equipped with an assortment of seeds as a matter of course. The seeds take up little room and gardening equipment can be made on the spot or is available nearly everywhere.

There is a great difference in the ordinary preparation of vegetables by the English and by us. The English usually boil their vegetables to a submissive, sticky pulp, in which the shape and, as some say, the flavor have long since been overcome. Our cooks do not cook their vegetables nearly so long, are apt to like them crisp. The English do not use nearly as many onions as we do and they use practically no garlic at all. The little gardens are a kind of symbol of revolt against foreign methods.

For example, the average English cook regards a vegetable with suspicion. It is his conviction that unless the vegetable is dominated and thoroughly convinced that it must offer no nonsense, it is likely either to revolt or to demand dominion status. Consequently, only those vegetables are encouraged which are docile and capable of learning English ways.

The brussels sprout is a good example of the acceptable vegetable. It is first allowed to become large and fierce. It is then picked from its stem and the daylights are boiled out of it. At the end of a few hours the little wild lump of green has disintegrated into a curious, grayish paste. It is then considered fit for consumption.

The same method is followed with cabbage. While the cabbage is boiling it is poked and beaten until, when it is served, it has given up its character and tastes exactly like brussels sprouts, which in turn taste like cabbage. Carrots are allowed to remain yellow but nothing else of their essential character is maintained.

No one has yet explained this innate fear the English suffer of a revolt of the vegetables. The easy-going American attitude of allowing the vegetable a certain amount of latitude short of the ballot is looked upon by the English as soft and degenerate. In the American gardens certain English spies have reported they have seen American soldiers pulling and eating raw carrots and turnips and onions.

It is strange to an American that the English, who love dogs and rarely eat them, nevertheless are brutal with vegetables. It is just one of those national differences which are unfathomable.

*   *

THE SHAPE OF THE WORLD

LONDON, *July 16, 1943*—This is no war, like other wars, to be won as other wars have been won. We remember the last war. It was a simple, easy thing. When we had destroyed the Kaiser and a little military clique, the evil thing was removed and all good things came into flower. It was not so, but the war was fought on that basis by troops who sang and then ran home for the millennium.

It is said that this is not a singing war and that is true. The soldiers fight and work under a load of worry. They know deeply that the destruction of the enemy is not the end of this war. And almost universally you find among the soldiers not a fear of the enemy but a fear of what is going to happen after the war. The collapse of retooled factories, the unemployment of millions due to the increase of automatic machinery, a depression that will make the last one look like a holiday.

They fight under a banner of four unimplemented freedoms —four words, and when anyone in authority tries to give these freedoms implements and methods the soldiers hear that man assaulted and dragged down. It doesn't matter whether the methods or the plans are good or bad. Any planning is assorted at home. And the troops feel they are going to come home to one of two things—either a painless anarchy, or a system set up in their absence with the cards stacked against them.

Ours is not a naïve Army. Common people have learned a great deal in the last twenty-five years, and the old magical words do not fool them any more. They do not believe the golden future made of words. They would like freedom from want. That means the little farm in Connecticut is safe from foreclosure. That means the job left when the soldier joined the Army is there waiting, and not only waiting but it will continue while the children grow up. That means there will be schools, and either savings to take care of illness in the family or medicine available without savings. Talking to many soldiers, it is the worry that comes out of them that is impressive. Is the country to be taken over by special interests through the medium of special pleaders? Is inflation to be permitted because a few people will grow rich through it? Are fortunes being made while these men get $50 a month? Will they go home to a country destroyed by greed? If anyone could assure them that these things are not true, or that, being true, they will not be permitted, then we would have a singing Army. This Army can defeat the enemy. There is no doubt about that. They know it and will accomplish it, but they do not want to go home to find a civil war in the making. The memory of the last depression is still fresh in their memories.

They remember the foreclosed farms, the slaughtered pigs to keep the prices up, the plowing under of the crops, because there was not intelligence enough in the leaders to devise a means of distributing an oversupply of food. They remember that every plan for general good life is dashed to pieces on the wall of necessary profits.

These things cannot be overstated. Anyone who can reassure these soldiers that such things will not happen again will put a weapon in their hands of incredible strength. What do the soldiers hear?—that Mr. Jones is calling Mr. Wallace names; that Mr. Jeffers is fighting with Mr. Ickes; czars of this and that are fighting for more power and more jurisdiction.

Congress, in a kind of hysteria of immunity from public criticism, has removed even the machinery of relief which might take up the impact of a new depression; black markets are flourishing and the operators are not little crooks, but the best people. The soldiers hear that the price of living is going up and wages are following them. A soldier is not a lone man. He usually has a family dependent to a large extent on the money he can allot, and his pay does not increase with the cost of living.

These are the things that he hears. The papers are full of it, the letters from home are full of it—quarreling, anxiety, greed. And, being a soldier, he cannot complain. He is forbidden to complain. You cannot have that kind of thing in an army. He is not cynical, but he is worried. He wants to get this war over with, and to get home to find what they have done to his country in his absence. The Four Freedoms define what he wants but unless some machinery, some foundation, some clear method is shown, he is likely to believe only in that freedom which Anatole France defined—the equal freedom of rich and poor to sleep under bridges.

*   *

THEATER PARTY

LONDON, *July 18, 1943*—It was late afternoon of the English summer and in one of London's innumerable outlying districts the motion-picture house was comfortably filled. There were some soldiers who had been wounded and were on their way to recovery. There were women of the services off duty for a few hours. Some civilian women were there for a quick picture after shopping and there were factory workers off shift. Down in front were rows of children, crowding as close to the screen as they could get.

It was just an average afternoon at the pictures. The house was comfortably filled but not crowded. In special places were some men in wheel chairs from the hospital. The picture was *I Married a Witch* with Veronica Lake—a fantasy comedy wherein a New England witch of Puritan times returns to life and falls straight into the traditional bedroom comedy—neither a distinguished piece of work nor a bad one. The children loved the picture and believed it because they believe all moving pictures.

Outside there was low cloud and it looked as though there might be rain later in the evening and there had not been enough rain.

While Veronica Lake, long blond hair over one eye, sat in pajamas on a man's bed and he worried for his good and respectable name and the children crowed with delight—ten German fighter-bombers whirled in over the coast. The spotters picked them up. The Spitfires took the air. The anti-aircraft guns fired and two of the raiders were shot down. A third crashed against a little hill. Then a crazy, ragged chase started in the gray cloud. Spitfires ranging and searching in the cloud. The raiders separated and lunged on toward London, and on the ground the sirens howled and the tremendous system of alarms and defenses went into action.

Only one of the raiders got through, twisting and dodging through the defenses. He came racing down out of the cloud and right under him was the theater. He was very low when he released his bombs. The top of the theater leaped into the air and then settled back into a rubble. The screen went blank. The raider banked his plane, whipped around, came back, and poured his guns into the wreck. Then he jerked his ship into the gray clouds and ran for the coast. And he left behind him the screaming of children in pain and fear.

The communities are organized for things like this. In a matter of minutes the rescue squads were at work; the firemen were on the ground. The squads are well trained. They forced themselves into the torn and shredded building. The broken children were carried out and rushed to the hospital, crushed and shot and destroyed. The dead ones were set aside for burial, but those who still breathed and kicked and whimpered went to the waiting doctors.

All night long the operations went on. Probing for bullets, hands and arms and legs cut off and put aside. Eyes removed. The anesthetists worked delicately against pain, dripping unconsciousness onto the masks. It went on through the night, the procession of the maimed to the hospital. The doctors worked carefully, speedily. Quick judgments—this one can't live—kept consciousness away. This one has a chance if both legs are sliced off. Judgments and quick work.

From the depots the blood plasma was rushed in and the strength from other people's veins dripped into the arteries of the children.

It was nine in the morning when the operating was finished. At the theater the tired squads were still finding a few bodies. And in the hospital beds—great wads of bandage and wide, staring, unbelieving eyes and utter weariness—the little targets, the seven-year-old military objectives.

Workmen were digging a great, long, common grave for the dead. Veronica Lake had flared up with the quick flash of burning film and only the reels she was wound on were left. And in the houses in the morning people were just beginning to be aware enough to cry. It was very quiet in the streets.

At a bar a tired doctor got a drink before he went to bed. His eyes were ringed with red sorrow and his hand shook as he lifted the whisky to his lips.

*   *

DIRECTED UNDERSTANDING

London, *July 19, 1943*—International amity, good fellowship, and mutual understanding between the British and Americans often reaches a pitch where war between the two seems very close. This is usually directed understanding, and it gives rise to some very silly situations.

Directed understanding and tolerance ordinarily begin with generalizations. Our troops approaching England are told in pamphlets what the British are like, where they are tender and where hard, what words, innocent at home, are harsh and ugly on the British ear. This has much the same effect as telling a friend, "You must meet Jones—wonderful fellow. You two will get along." With a start like that, Jones has got two strikes on him before you ever meet him. He has to live down being a charming fellow before you can tolerate him. In this case it is even worse, because the British are told that they will like us when they just get to know us. The result is that the two come together like strange dogs, each one looking for trouble.

It takes a long time to live down this kind of understanding.

The second phase of getting along is carried on in innumerable attempts to describe each other. The British are so and so. The Americans are so and so. The British are just like other people only more so. The Americans are boasters who love money. This love of money is, of course, unique with Americans. Every other people detests money. The Americans are fine, sturdy people. The British are fine, sturdy people. This is obviously a lie. There are good ones and stinkers on both sides. Setting them up doesn't do any good. Just about the time you get a liking and a respect for a number of Englishmen, someone comes along and tells you about the English and you have to start from scratch again. This same thing, undoubtedly, happens to the English too.

The third little pitfall concerns the qualities of the fighting men. A big, rangy old mountain boy comes rolling down the street with his knuckles just barely clearing the pavement, and right behind is a Guardsman, shoulders back, chin up, nine buttons glowing like mad. Immediately the comparison is made. One is a fine soldier and the other is a lout. The fact of the matter is that they are both covering ground at the same rate, and each one could probably cover the same ground with a full pack. And then, having learned about soldierly qualities, you see a little twist-faced, wide-shouldered Tommy who walks sideways like a crab, and you realize that he's as good a fighting man as the world has produced, but on his record, not on his soldierly bearing.

The whole trouble seems to lie in generalities. Once you have made a generality you are stuck with it. You have to defend it. Let's say the British and/or American soldier is a superb soldier. The British and/or American officer is a gentleman. You start in with a lie. There are good ones and bad ones. You find out for yourself which is which if you can be let alone. And when you see an American second lieutenant misbehaving in a London club, it is expected that you will deny it. Or if you meet an ill-mannered, surly popinjay of a British officer, the British are expected to deny that he exists. But he does exist, and they hate him as much as we do. The trouble with generalities, particularly patriotic ones, is that they force people to defend things they don't normally like at all.

It must be a great shock to an Englishman who is convinced that Americans are boasters when he meets a modest one. His sense of rightness is outraged. Preconceived generalities are bad enough without trying consciously to start new ones. Recently a Georgia boy with a face like a catfish and the fine soldierly bearing of a coyote complained bitterly that he had been here four days and hadn't seen a duke. He had got to believing that there weren't any dukes and he was shocked beyond words.

Somewhere there is truth or an approximation of it. If there is an engagement and the British say, "We got knocked about a bit," and the Americans say, "They shot the hell out of us," neither statement is true. Understatement is universally admired here and overstatement is detested, whereas neither one is near the truth and neither one had anything to do with the fighting quality of the soldier involved. We know that you can't say the Americans are something or other when those Americans are crackers and long-legged men from the Panhandle and the neat business men in bifocals and shoddy jewelry salesmen and high riggers from the woods in Oregon. And it is just as silly to try to describe the British when they are Lancashiremen and Welshmen and cockneys and Liverpool longshoremen. We get along very well as individuals, but just the moment we become the Americans and they become the British trouble is not far behind.

*   *

BIG TRAIN

LONDON, *July 25, 1943*—Private Big Train Mulligan, after induction and training and transfer overseas, found himself, with a minimum of goldbricking, in a motor pool in London, the driver of a brown Army Ford, and likely to take any kind of officers anywhere. It is not a job the Big Train dislikes. He drives generals or lieutenants where he is told to drive them at the speed he is told to drive them. Leaves them. Waits. Picks them up. You have only to tell him what time you want to get there and he will have you there, and although the strain on you and pedestrians and wandering dogs and cats will be great, Big Train will not be affected at all.

In his position he probably knows more military secrets than anyone in the European theater of operations. But he explains, "Mostly I don't listen. If I do, it goes in one ear and out the other. I've got other things to think about." He has arrived at a certain philosophy regarding the Army and his private life. About promotion he has this to say: "If you want to be a general, then it's all right for you to take stripes, but if you figure that maybe you personally can't win the war, then you're better off as a private and you have more fun." He doesn't like to order other people about any more than he likes to be ordered about. He can't avoid the second, but he gets around the first by just staying a private. "Not that I'd mind," he said. "I'd take the hooks for a job like this, but I don't want to tell a bunch of men what to do."

Having decided (1) that he couldn't win the war single-handed, (2) that the war was going to last quite a long time, (3) that he wasn't going to get home on any given day, and (4) what the hell anyways, the Big Train settled down to enjoy what he couldn't resist.

He probably knows England as well as any living American. He knows the little towns, the by-roads, north and south, and he has what is generally considered the best address book in Europe. He talks to everyone and never forgets a name or address. The result of this is that when he deposits his colonel, two majors, and a captain at some sodden little hotel in a damp little town, there to curse the beds and the food, when the Big Train gets dismissed for the night he consults his address book. Then he visits one of the many friends he has made here and there.

The Big Train gets a piece of meat and fresh garden vegetables for supper. He drinks toasts to his friends. He sleeps in clean white sheets and in the morning he breakfasts on new-laid eggs. Exactly on time he arrives at the sodden little hotel. The colonel and the majors are exhausted from having fought lumps in their beds all night. Their digestions are ruined by the doughy food, but the Big Train is rested and thriving. He is alert and eventually will leave his officers in another tavern and find a friend for lunch.

The Big Train is not what you call handsome, but he is pleasant-looking and soft-spoken and he particularly likes the company of women, the casual company or any other kind. He just feels happy if there is a girl to talk to. How he finds them no one has ever been able to discover. You can leave the Big Train parked in the middle of a great plain, with no buildings and no brush, no nothing, and when you come back ten minutes later there will be a girl sitting in the seat beside him, smoking the colonel's cigarettes and chewing a piece of the major's gum, while the Big Train carefully writes down her address and the town she comes from.

His handling of women and girls is neither wolfish nor subtle. It consists in his being genuinely interested in them. He speaks to them with a kind of affectionate courtesy. Is a stickler for decorum of all kinds. He addresses all women, whether he knows them or not, as "dear" and he manages to make it convincing, probably because it is true. The result is that the women always want to see him again and, if the war lasts long enough, this wish will be granted in time. Mulligan is perfectly honest. If he should give the colonel's cigarettes to the girl, a whole package of them, he explains this fact to the colonel and agrees to replace them as soon as he gets back to London. The colonel invariably refuses to consider such a thing, as being ungallant on his part. Of course the girl should have his cigarettes. He puts the girl at her ease, a place she has never left. Goggles at her, puffs out his chest, and drives away. But Big Train knows where she lives and who lives with her and he has already calculated what he will be likely to have for dinner when he calls on her.

About the English the Big Train has terse and simple ideas. "I get on all right with the ones I like and I don't have nothing to do with the ones I don't like. It was just the same at home," he says. It is probable that he has more good effect on Anglo-American relations than two hundred government propagandists striving to find the fundamental differences between the nations. Big Train is not aware of many differences except in accent and liquor. He likes the ones he likes and he refuses to like for any reason whatever a man he wouldn't like at home.

His speech is picturesque. He refers to a toothy, smiling girl as looking like a jackass eating bumblebees. He refuses to worry about the war. "When they want me to do that let them pin stars on my shoulders," he says. "That's what we got generals for." Big Train Mulligan, after two years in the Army and one year overseas, is probably one of the most relaxed and most successful privates the war has seen. When they want him to take up his rifle and fight he is quite willing to do so, but until someone suggests it, he is not going to worry about it. There are good little dinners waiting for him in nice little cottages all over England. And so long as the colonel's cigarettes hold out the Big Train will not leave his hostess empty-handed.

*   *

BOB HOPE

LONDON, *July 26, 1943*—When the time for recognition of service to the nation in wartime comes to be considered, Bob Hope should be high on the list. This man drives himself and is driven. It is impossible to see how he can do so much, can cover so much ground, can work so hard, and can be so effective. He works month after month at a pace that would kill most people.

Moving about the country in camps, airfields, billets, supply depots, and hospitals, you hear one thing consistently. Bob Hope is coming, or Bob Hope has been here. The Secretary of War is on an inspection tour, but it is Bob Hope who is expected and remembered.

In some way he has caught the soldiers' imagination. He gets laughter wherever he goes from men who need laughter. He has created a character for himself—that of the man who tries too hard and fails, and who boasts and is caught at it. His wit is caustic, but it is never aimed at people, but at conditions and at ideas, and where he goes men roar with laughter and repeat his cracks for days afterward.

Hope does four, sometimes five, shows a day. In some camps the men must come in shifts because they cannot all hear him at the same time. Then he jumps into a car, rushes to the next post, and because he broadcasts and everyone listens to his broadcasts, he cannot use the same show more than a few times. He must, in the midst of his rushing and playing, build new shows constantly. If he did this for a while and then stopped and took a rest it would be remarkable, but he never rests. And he has been doing this ever since the war started. His energy is boundless.

Hope takes his shows all over. It isn't only to the big camps. In little groups on special duty you hear the same thing. Bob Hope is coming on Thursday. They know weeks in advance that he is coming. It would be rather a terrible thing if he did not show up. Perhaps that is some of his drive. He has made some kind of contract with himself and with the men that nobody, least of all Hope, could break. It is hard to over-estimate the importance of this thing and the responsibility involved.

The battalion of men who are moving half-tracks from one place to another, doing a job that gets no headlines, no public notice, and yet which must be done if there is to be a victory, are forgotten, and they feel forgotten. But Bob Hope is in the country. Will he come to them, or won't he? And then one day they get a notice that he is coming. Then they feel remembered. This man in some way has become that kind of bridge. It goes beyond how funny he can be or how well Frances Langford sings. It has been interesting to see how he has become a symbol.

This writer, not knowing Hope, can only conjecture what goes on inside the man. He has seen horrible things and has survived them with good humor and made them more bearable, but that doesn't happen without putting a wound on a man. He is cut off from rest, and even from admitting weariness. Having become a symbol, he must lead a symbol life.

Probably the most difficult, the most tearing thing of all, is to be funny in a hospital. The long, low buildings are dispersed in case they should be attacked. Working in the gardens, or reading in the lounge rooms are the ambulatory cases in maroon bathrobes. But in the wards, in the long aisles of pain the men lie, with eyes turned inward on themselves, and on their people. Some are convalescing with all the pain and itch of convalescence. Some work their fingers slowly, and some cling to the little trapezes which help them to move in bed.

The immaculate nurses move silently in the aisles at the foot of the beds. The time hangs very long. Letters, even if they came every day, would seem weeks apart. Everything that can be done is done, but medicine cannot get at the lonesomeness and the weakness of men who have been strong. And nursing cannot shorten one single endless day in a hospital bed. And Bob Hope and his company must come into this quiet, inward, lonesome place, and gently pull the minds outward and catch the interest, and finally bring laughter up out of the black water. There is a job. It hurts many of the men to laugh, hurts knitting bones, strains at sutured incisions, and yet the laughter is a great medicine.

This story is told in one of those nameless hospitals which must be kept safe from bombs. Hope and company had worked and gradually they got the leaden eyes to sparkling, had planted and nurtured and coaxed laughter to life. A gunner, who had a stomach wound, was gasping softly with laughter. A railroad casualty slapped the cast on his left hand with his right hand by way of applause. And once the laughter was alive, the men laughed before the punch line and it had to be repeated so they could laugh again.

Finally it came time for Frances Langford to sing. The men asked for "As Time Goes By." She stood up beside the little GI piano and started to sing. Her voice is a little hoarse and strained. She has been working too hard and too long. She got through eight bars and was into the bridge, when a boy with a head wound began to cry. She stopped, and then went on, but her voice wouldn't work any more, and she finished the song whispering and then she walked out, so no one could see her, and broke down. The ward was quiet and no one applauded. And then Hope walked into the aisle between the beds and he said seriously, "Fellows, the folks at home are having a terrible time about eggs. They can't get any powdered eggs at all. They've got to use the old-fashioned kind that you break open."

There's a man for you—there is really a man.

*   *

A COZY CASTLE

LONDON, *July 27, 1943*—The jeep turns off the main road and pulls to a stop. The great gate of gray stone arches over the driveway. When it was built America was a wilderness with a few colonies clinging passionately to its edges. From the stone sentry room an American sentry emerges and stands by the jeep. He looks at passes. He salutes and opens a huge iron gate.

The jeep moves on into an ascending driveway overarched with oaks and beeches six feet through the trunks. The road curves and climbs a little hill and ahead you can see a gray tower poking above the enormous trees. Then you come out of the neat, ancient forest and there is a perfect castle against a hill, with lawns in front of it. It is a little castle, only about forty rooms, a cottage for its period. And it was built by a certain English king for a certain English mistress.

It is odd that this ancient scandal must not be identified but it is so. If, for instance, it were known which king and which mistress were involved in the building of the little castle, then it would be known by the enemy which castle it is and if, further, it were known that American troops are quartered in this castle, it would become a target for enemy aircraft. But since a wholesome number of English kings had mistresses and built little castles for them, so much information does not give the enemy a target or rather it gives him a number of targets too great to concentrate on.

On the lawn in front of the castle, where once perhaps gentlemen in heavy armor challenged one another with spears, a platoon of American soldiers, helmeted and with full packs, are doing close-order drill, marching, counter-marching, opening and closing ranks, their bayonets gleaming in the summer English sunshine.

In the gardens leading to the pointed door the roses are blooming. Red roses and white roses. Great-grandchildren of the bushes from which perhaps the symbols of Lancaster and York were picked and worn as insignia in the Civil War. The stones of the entrance are deeply worn, concave as basins, and beyond is a dark hall, so high and shadow-deep in the midday that you must get your eyes used to it before you can see the carved oaken ceiling from which thousands of little oak faces look out. And in this great hall an American Army sergeant sits behind a pine table and does his work.

Beyond, through an open door, is an even larger room but this one is lighter, for one side of it has large leaded windows, constructed in diamonds and lozenges and circles and moons of glass. And this also looks on the rose garden, the lawn, and finally to the forest.

There is a great fireplace in this room, a fireplace so high that a tall man can walk inside without stooping and could lie down without scrunching. The mantel over the fireplace is deep with heraldic carving. This is the lounge. On chairs procured somewhere the GIs sit and read and listen to the radio. A fine bar has been built against one wall, where Coca-Cola and pop are sold. And overhead, the arching roof of carved oak, chiseled and fitted long before America was born. And a soldier leaning back in his chair is staring fascinated at the ceiling. There is a copy of *Yank* in his lap. He squints his eyes and studies the ceiling. He withdraws his attention and calls, "Hey, Walter, have the Dodgers got twenty-four or twenty-five games?"

Up the broad stairway is a gallery and then the thirty rooms or so in which the guests of the couple were made comfortable, for it is probable that only five or six hundred people knew about this old scandal, including the lady's husband. The rooms are large, and each one has its carved fireplace and its little leaded, diamond-paned window, looking dimly on the gardens. But the rooms themselves are squad rooms with the cots arranged in a line, the shoes at attention underneath, the lockers with drawn-up blouses and trousers and towels and the helmets squarely on top. The rooms are probably much cleaner than they were when the king's mistress lived there.

Downstairs in a kind of cave is the kitchen, where an Army cook is baking square apple pies by the quarter-acre. The floor is so deeply worn that he has to step over some of the high places. His coal stove is roaring, and he has arrived at that quiet hopelessness that cooks get on finally realizing that their work is never going to be finished, that there is no way of feeding a man once for all.

The CO of the post is a first lieutenant from Texas and the second in command is a Chicago second lieutenant. They are young and stern and friendly. The job of keeping the castle in order is just a job to them.

There is no point to any of this except the change of pageantry. The place, which was built for heralds and courtiers, for soldiers in body armor, is in no way outraged by the new thing. The jeeps and armored cars, the half-tracks that come in through the gates, the helmeted soldiers on the lawn do not seem out of place. They belong here. They are probably very little different from the earlier inhabitants. Certainly the king in question would have been glad for them, because he had his international troubles too.

*   *

THE YANKS ARRIVE

LONDON, *July 28, 1943*—The little gray English station is set in the green, rolling fields where the grass is being cut and, where the mowing machine has gone, the cut grass is wilting and the red poppies are wilting. The double tracks go by the front of the station and a "Y" siding runs in back of the station. At 4:03 the American commandant and four officers drive to the station. A British officer comes out of the signalman's room. "The train will be four minutes late," he says. All the officers look at their watches. On the main line a through train roars through at about seventy miles an hour. The young lieutenant says, "I thought British trains were slow."

"They used to hold the world's record for speed," the commandant says.

On another track a freight train moves rapidly through the station. The flat cars are loaded with tanks, a solid line of tanks the whole length of the train. A hundred yards from the station a clubmobile is parked, a bus converted into a kitchen for the cooking of doughnuts and coffee and run by two Red Cross girls. Their coffee urns are steaming and great baskets of doughnuts are accumulating. They lift out the doughnuts and load the baskets with them. On top of the bus is a loudspeaker connected with a phonograph.

The commandant says, "That big girl is a great one. We got five hundred men at six o'clock this morning. They were pretty tired. That big girl put on a record and did a Highland fling to some hot music. She's a funny one." The smell of the cooking doughnuts comes down the breeze.

The British officer comes out of the signalman's house again. "It will be here in three minutes," he says. And again the officers look at their watches. The little train comes around the bend. It passes the station, puts its tail into the "Y," and backs into the siding. The compartments are solid with helmeted men and their equipment is piled in front of them to the knees. Their faces are almost as brown as their uniforms. They are sitting with their packs on. It is a hot afternoon, one of the few of the summer.

As the train pulls in, the phonograph in the clubmobile howls, "Mr. Five by Five." The sound carries a long way. The soldiers turn their heads slowly and look toward the music. Now a sergeant runs down the side of the train and opens the doors of the compartments but the men do not move. A stout captain, with a very black mustache, shouts, "All right, men. Pile out of it." And the little compartments disgorge the men. They stand helplessly on the platform, their shoulders damp with sweat under the pack straps and their backs wet under the packs. They carry their barracks bags too and the things which won't go in, a guitar here, and a mandolin, a pair of shoes. One man has a mongrel fox terrier on a string and it stands beside him panting with excitement.

The stout, worried captain gets the men lined up and marches them to the clubmobile. Swing music is still shrieking from the loudspeaker on the roof. A single file of men passes a little counter on a side of the truck and each one gets a big cup of coffee and two doughnuts Then they break their ranks and stand about drinking the coffee and looking lost. The big girl comes out of the truck and works on them.

"Where you from, boy?"

"Michigan."

"Why, we're neighbors. I come from Illinois."

A local wolf, a slicker at home, a dark boy with sideburns, says wearily and just from a sense of duty, "What you doing tonight, baby?"

"What are you doing?" the big girl asks, and the men about laugh loudly as if it were very funny.

The tired wolf puts an arm about her waist. "Plant me," he says, and the two do a grotesque shag, a kind of slow-motion jitterbug.

A blond boy with a sunburned nose and red eyelids shyly approaches a lieutenant. He has his coffee in one hand and his two doughnuts in the other. Too late he realizes that he is in trouble. He balances the two doughnuts on the edge of his cup and they promptly fall into the coffee. He salutes and the lieutenant returns it gravely.

"Excuse me, sir," the boy says. "Aren't you a movie star?"

"I used to be," the lieutenant says. "I used to be."

"I knew I'd seen you in pictures," the boy says. "I'll write home about seeing you here. Say," he says with excitement, "would you write your name here on something and I could send it home and then they'd have to believe me and they could keep it for me."

"Sure," the lieutenant says, and he signs his name with a pencil on the back of a grubby envelope from the soldier's pocket. The boy regards it for a moment.

"What're you doing here?" he asks.

"Why, I'm just in the Army, the same as you are."

"Oh, yes, of course. Yes, I see you are. Well, they'll have to believe I saw you now."

"How long have you been over?" the lieutenant asks.

"We're not supposed to say anything about stuff like that."

"Sure, I forgot. Good boy to remember it."

The doughnuts in the coffee have become semi-liquid by now. The boy drinks the coffee and the doughnuts without noticing.

"Do you suppose we'll ever be let to go to London?" he asks.

"Sure. When you get a pass."

"Well, that's a long way off, isn't it?"

"Not so far. You could make it on a forty-eight-hour pass easy and have lots of time."

"Well. Are there lots of girls there?"

"Sure. Plenty."

"And will they, will they talk to a guy?"

"Sure they will."

"Hot damn!" says the boy. "Oh, hot damn!"

"Fall in," the stout, worried captain shouts, and, "Fall in," the sergeants shout. The blond boy gets in line, still holding his cup. The big girl yells at him over the music, "Hey, sonny. We need those cups."

She rushes fiercely up to him and grabs the cup and then quickly pats him once on the shoulder. The men on both sides of him laugh loudly, as if it were very funny.

*　　　　*

A HAND

LONDON, *July 29, 1943*—The soldier wears a maroon bathrobe and pajamas and slippers, the uniform of the Army hospital. He is a little pale and shaky, the way convalescents are. His left arm he carries crooked and high, and the fingers of his left hand hook over helplessly. In front of him on a table is a half-built model of a Liberator. Not covered yet, but a mass of tiny struts and ribs and braces. And he has a sheet of balsa wood, stamped with the patterns, and he has a razor blade and a little bowl of glue, with a match sticking out of it.

"I got hurt in Africa," he says. "Got hit in the stomach, but they fixed that up pretty good." He holds up his left arm. "This is what bothers me," he says. "That was broke awful bad. I haven't been out of a cast long." He moves the fingers slightly.

"Not much feeling in them," he says. "I can't make a fist. I can't grab ahold of anything. At least, I couldn't. It's kind of numb.

"I got hold of this model," he says. "I can hold things down with my hand, like this." He puts the side of his hand down on the sheet of balsa. "I did all of that with my right hand. I guess it's lucky I'm right-handed." He regards his left hand and moves the fingers. "The doctor says I'll be able to use it to grab hold of things if I just exercise it. But it's hard to exercise it when you can just barely feel it's there.

"A funny thing happened yesterday," he says. "Here, I'll show you the exact place." He takes a pencil and sticks it into the maze of tiny braces. "There, you see that piece in there? The one with the little pencil mark on it? I marked it so I'd remember which one it was.

"Yesterday I was trying to get that set in right, and you can see it's a hard place to get at. You've got to hold it here and work it up under. Well, I didn't even know I was doing it. I came to, and I was holding that little piece in my left hand." He regards the wizened finger with amazement. "I told the doctor about it and he said that was all right and I should try to use it every bit I could. Well, sir, when I think about it I can't do it. Not yet, anyway. Maybe I can later, a little bit at a time. I roll a pencil under my fingers. They say that's a good thing to do. I can feel it some, too."

He holds a sheet of balsa pattern down with the side of his left hand and with a razor blade carefully cuts out the tiny curved piece he is going to use next. It is an intricate piece, and his hand shakes a little, but the razor blade runs through on the black line, and he lifts the little piece free and puts it down on the table to apply a spot of glue to each end of it. Then carefully, with his right hand, he sets the piece in its place. "I let my nails grow long," he says. "I can use my fingernails for lots of things." With the long fingernail of his right forefinger he scrapes off a little drop of glue that is squeezed out of the joint and wipes it on a piece of paper.

"I'm worried about this hand," he says. "Of course, I guess I can get a job. I'm not worried about that so much. I can always get a job. But I've got to get this hand into shape so that it will grab ahold of things." He turns the model plane over and then studies the pattern sheet for the next piece. He is silent for a long time. "My wife knows I was hurt. She doesn't know how bad. She knows I'm going to get well all right and come home, but—she must be thinking pretty hard. I got to get that hand working. She wouldn't like a cripple with a hand that wouldn't work."

His eyes are a little feverish. "Well, how would you like a cripple to come home? What would you think about that?

"It will always be a little crooked," he says, "but I wouldn't mind that so much if it worked. I don't think she would mind so much if it worked. She has got a job in a plane factory out on the Coast—doing a man's work. She says she is doing fine and I'm not to worry. Here. I'll show you a picture of her." He reaches in his bathrobe pocket. "Where is it?" he says. "The nurse always puts it in here." He puts his left hand in his pocket and brings out a little leather wallet. And suddenly he sees what he has done and the fingers relax and the wallet drops to the table. "God Almighty!" he says. "Did you see that?" He looks at the crooked hand still suspended in the air. "That's twice in two days," he says softly. "Twice in two days."

*   *

THE CAREER OF BIG TRAIN MULLIGAN

SOMEWHERE IN ENGLAND, *August 4, 1943*—It has been possible to compile further data on the life and methods of Private Big Train Mulligan, a man who has succeeded in making a good part of the Army work for him. It has been said of him by one of his enemies, of whom he has very few, that he would be a goldbrick but he is too damn lazy.

In a course of close study, extending over several days, certain qualities have stood out in the private in addition to those mentioned in the previous report. Big Train has a very curious method. If you are not very careful, you find yourself carrying his luggage and you never know how it happened. Recently, in one of the minor crises which are an everyday occurrence to Big Train, this writer came out of a kind of a haze of friendship to find that he had not only lent Mulligan £2 10s, but had forced it on him without security and had, furthermore, emerged from the transaction with a sense of having been honored. How this was accomplished is anybody's guess. Sometime in the future, no doubt, Mulligan will pay this money back, but in such a manner that it will seem that he has been robbed.

Mulligan has carried looting, requisitioning, whatever you want to call it, to its highest point. He is a firm believer in the adage that an army moves on its stomach, a position he rather likes. He loves nice foods and he usually gets them. A few days ago a party was visiting a ship which had recently put into a port in England with war materials. The party went to the bridge, met the master and the other officers, drank a small cup of very good coffee, and ate a quarter-ounce of cookies, conversing politely the while. On coming back to the dock where the car stood and where Mulligan should conceivably be on duty, of course, no such thing was true.

Mulligan was not in sight. One of this party who has known the private and admired him for some time remarked, "If I were to look for Mulligan right now I should find the icebox on that ship with a good deal of confidence that Mulligan would not be far from it." Accordingly, the party found its way to the ship's refrigerator and there was Mulligan, leaning jauntily back against a table. He was holding the thickest roast-beef sandwich imaginable in his hand. He has learned to eat very rapidly while talking on all subjects. He never misses a bite or a word. His pace seems slow but his execution is magnificent. Not between bites but during bites he was telling an admiring circle, made up of a steward and three naval gunners, a story of rapine and other amusements which completely distracted them from noticing that Big Train had a foot-high stack of sandwiches behind him on the table.

The senior officer said, "Mulligan, don't you think it is about time we went along?"

Mulligan said, "Yes, sir. I was just coming along but I thought the captain might be a little hungry. I was just getting a snack ready for the captain." He reached behind him and brought out the great pile of roast-beef sandwiches, which he passed about. Now, whether these sandwiches had been prepared for just such an emergency or whether Mulligan had intended to eat them himself will never be known. We prefer to believe that it was just as he said. Mulligan is a thoughtful friend and an unselfish man. Besides this, he never goes into a blind alley. He has always a line of retreat, which simply proves that he is a good soldier.

Should his officer be faint with hunger, Mulligan has a piece of chocolate to tide the captain over. What difference that the chocolate belonged to the captain in the first place and he was led to believe that it was all gone? The fact of the matter is that when he needs his own chocolate Mulligan is happy to give him half of it.

The Big Train has been in England now something over a year and he has acquired a speech which can only be described as Georgia-Oxford. He addresses people as "mate" or even "mait." He refuses to learn that he cannot get petrol at a gas station but he refers to lifts and braces.

Many an officer has tried to get Mulligan promoted to a corporalcy, if only to have something to break him from, but he is firmly entrenched in his privacy. There is nothing you can do to Mulligan except put him in jail and then you have no one to drive you. If he were a corporal you could break him, but Mulligan has so far circumvented any such move on the part of his superiors. When the recommendation has gone in, at just the right moment he has been guilty of some tiny infraction of the rules—not much, but just enough to make it impossible to promote him. His car is a little bit dirty at inspection. Mulligan does six hours' full-pack drill and is safe from promotion for a good time.

Mulligan has nearly everything he wants—women, leisure, travel, and companionship. He wants only one thing and he is trying to work out a way to get it. He would like a dog, preferably a Scottie, and he would like to take it in his car with him. So far he has not worked out his method, but it is a foregone conclusion that he will not only get his dog but that his officer will feed it, and when Mulligan has a date in the evening his officer will probably take care of the dog for him and will feel very good about it, too. The Army is a perfect setting for this Mulligan. He would be foolish ever to leave it. And he is rarely foolish.

*   *

CHEWING GUM

LONDON, *August 6, 1943*—At the port the stevedores are old men. The average age is fifty-two, and these men handle the cargo from America. Their pace does not seem fast, but the cargo gets unloaded and away. The only men on the docks anywhere near military age who are not in uniform are the Irish from the neutral Free State, who are not subject to Army call. They stay pretty much to themselves; for while they may approve of their neutrality, it is not pleasant to be a neutral in a country at war. They feel outsiders.

Little old Welshmen with hard, grooved faces handle the cargo. There is a shrunken man directing the big crane. He stands beside the open hatch and with his hands directs the cargo slings as though he were directing an orchestra. Palm down and the fingers fluttering brings down the sling. Palm up raises it, and by the tempo of his motions the operator knows whether to go slowly or rapidly. This man has a thin, high voice which nevertheless cuts through the noise of the pounding engine and grinding gears. His fingers flutter upward and the locomotive rises into the air on the end of a sling. The man seems to waft it over the side with his hands. Eighty-seven tons of locomotive, and he lowers it to the tracks on the docks with his hands.

On an imaginary line the children stand and watch the cargo come out. They are not permitted to go beyond their line for fear they might be hurt. There are at least a hundred of them, a little shabby, as everyone in England is after four years of war. And not too clean, for they have been playing on ground that is largely coal dust. How they cluster about an American soldier who has come off the ship! They want gum. Much as the British may deplore the gum-chewing habit, their children find it delightful. There are semi-professional gum beggars among the children. "Penny, mister?" has given way to "Goom, mister?"

When you have gum you have something permanent, something you can use day after day and even trade when you are tired of it. Candy is ephemeral. One moment you have candy, and the next moment you haven't. But gum is really property.

The grubby little hands are held up to the soldier and the chorus swells. "Goom, mister?"

"I don't have any," the soldier says, but they pay no attention to that. "Goom, mister?" they shriek and crowd in closer. A steward comes down the gangplank from the ship. He is a little tipsy and he is dressed for the town. He is going to have a time for himself. A few children go to him and test him out. "Goom, mister?" they ask. The steward grins genially, pulls a handful of coins from his pocket and throws them into the air. The dust rises and covers a little riot, and when it clears the steward is in full flight with the pack baying after him.

Only one small boy has stayed with the soldier—a very little boy with blond hair and gray eyes. He holds the soldier's hand and the soldier blushes with pleasure. "Is it as nice in America as it is here?" the boy asks.

"No—it's just about the same as here," the soldier says. "It's bigger, but just about the same."

"I guess you really have no goom?"

"No, not a piece."

"Is there much goom in America?"

"Oh, yes, lots of it."

The little boy sighs deeply. "I'll go there sometime," he says gravely.

The pack returns slowly. They have lost their quarry and are looking for new game. Then over the side the garbage is lowered in a large box. It is golden with squeezed orange skins. The children hesitate, because it is against all their training to break rules. But the test is too great. They can't stand it. They break over the line and tumble on the garbage box. They squeeze the skins for the last drop of juice that may conceivably be there.

A bobby comes up quickly, his high hat making him seem a foot taller than he is. "Get ahn naow, get ahn," he says mildly.

The rebels cram the skins into their pockets and then, dutifully, they go back to their boundary, but their pockets bulge with the loot.

"That's naught naice," the bobby says. "But they do get very 'ungry for horanges. They really do. I 'aven't 'ad a horange in four years. It's the law; no one hover five years old can 'ave a horange.

"They need them most, you see," he explained.

*　　　　*

MUSSOLINI

LONDON, *August 9, 1943*—The ship was in mid-ocean when Mussolini resigned. Rumor ran among the soldiers and the crew and the Army nurses that something important had happened. Then, down from the bridge, came the corroboration—"Mussolini has resigned"—on that. For five days the people on board had that for their minds and their hopes to play with. And the process went something like this:

Two sergeants and a PFC stood out of the wind in the lee

of a life raft. "Well, you've got to admit it's good news if it's true," the PFC said.

"Yes," said the technical sergeant, "but you know how it is when a guy is quitting. He gets kicked in the pants. There must be plenty of people who would like to take a sock at old Musso. I wouldn't be surprised if he didn't live too long."

"You got right," the staff sergeant said. "I'd hate to be in Musso's shoes."

The ship plowed through the sea and the escorts hovered about like worried chickens. . . .

A second lieutenant sat in the lounge, talking to an Army nurse. "Gin rummy?" he asked.

"Sure," said the nurse.

The lieutenant leaned toward her. "A private in my outfit got it pretty straight. Somebody knocked off the Duce."

"How do you mean?"

The second lieutenant shuffled and passed the deck for cut. "Got him. That's what I mean. Cut his throat. I hope he bled some."

The nurse ignored the cards. She frowned. "I wonder whether he really had power or whether he was just a figure-head."

"Why? What difference does it make if he's dead?"

"Well," said the nurse, "if he had power, then the Fascists go out with him gone. They'll all get killed. They'll all get killed. There'll be a revolution. That's what I mean."

"I guess you're right," said the lieutenant. "You want to keep score . . . ?"

The captain lay on his back in his bunk in the crowded stateroom. He talked to the bunk above him. "You've got to hand it to those Wops," he said. "When they've got something to fight for, they sure put up a fight."

A major's head appeared over the edge of the upper bunk. "What are you talking about?"

"Didn't you hear? After Mussolini got bumped off, the Wops revolted. They've got the nicest little revolution going you ever heard. Rome is a shambles. They're hunting down the Fascists like rats."

"God Almighty," said the major, "this would be the right time to invade. From a military point of view, you couldn't ask for a better time. I wonder if we've got the stuff ready to do it?"

A steward lingered in the passageway near the icebox. A KP came furtively near. "Stay out of those strawberries," the steward said sternly.

"We ain't got no strawberries," said the furtive one. "The nurses went through them strawberries like we're going through Italy. I didn't get none of them strawberries."

"Have we got into Italy?"

"Got in? Where you been? We're halfway up the calf right now. There's MPs walkin' the streets of Rome this minute and the Wops puttin' flowers in their hair."

The captain interrupted the sleepy poker game. "We've got to have a drink on this," he said. "Who's got some whisky?"

"Don't be silly," said a lieutenant colonel. "We haven't had any whisky since the second day out. What are you drinking to? The invasion of Italy?"

"Invasion, hell. Italy is in our hands."

"I've got a bottle," said the lieutenant colonel, and he climbed over legs and dug in his briefcase. They stood together and clinked the glasses and tossed off the whisky. The captain turned and threw his glass out of the porthole. "That's a pretty important drink," he said. "I wouldn't want any common drink to get into that glass." He peered out the porthole. "A seagull picked us up. We can't be very far out," he said.

The lieutenant colonel said, "You know, with Italy out, Germany is going to have a time holding the Balkans down. They're going to want to get out from under. I bet Greece revolts, too. And Turkey was about ready to come in. This may be the push she needs." . . .

Three GIs sat in a windblown cave, made by slinging their shelter halves between a rail and a davit and a ventilator. They watched the whitecaps go surging by. "I'd like to get there before it's over, Willie. I won't get a chance to see any action if we don't hurry up."

"You'll see plenty action and you'll tote plenty bales before you're through, brother."

"I don't know about that. With those Turks running wild, Germany can't hold out forever. Why, Germany's so busy now, I'll bet we could even get in across the Channel. This is a slow damn scow." . . .

"Gentlemen," said a twenty-year-old lieutenant to three other twenty-year-old lieutenants, "gentlemen, I give you Paris."

"My old man took Paris in the last war," said one of the gentlemen.

"Gentlemen," said the first speaker, his voice shaking, "we've crossed the Channel. Oh, boy, oh, boy! We're in."

The three joined hands in a kind of fraternal cat's cradle. . . .

And so the ship came into port with the war fought and won. It took them a little time to get over it.

*   *

CRAPS

LONDON, *August 12, 1943*—This is one of Mulligan's lies and it concerns a personality named Eddie. Mulligan has soldiered with Eddie and knows him well. Gradually it becomes apparent that Mulligan has soldiered with nearly everyone of importance.

At any rate this Eddie was a crap shooter, but of such a saintly character that his integrity in the use of the dice was never questioned. Eddie was just lucky, so lucky that he could flop the dice against the wall and bounce them halfway across the barracks floor on a Sunday and still make a natural.

From performances like this the suspicion grew that Eddie had the ear of some force a little more than human. Eddie, over a period of a year or two, became a rich and happy man, not so lucky in love, but you can't have everything. It was Eddie's contention that the dice could get him a woman any time, but he never saw a woman who could make him roll naturals. Sour grapes though this may have been, Eddie abode by it.

Came the time finally when Eddie and his regiment were put on board a ship and started off for X. It wasn't a very large ship, and it was very crowded. Decks and staterooms and alleys, all crowded. And it just happened that the ship sailed within reasonable time of payday.

That first day there were at least two hundred crap games on the deck, and while Eddie got into one, he did it listlessly, just to keep his hand in, and not to tire himself, because he knew that the important stuff was coming later. Between the chicken games Eddie moped about and did a good deed or two to get himself into a state of grace he knew was necessary later. He helped to carry a "B" bag for a slightly tipsy GI and reluctantly accepted a pint of bourbon, which canceled out the good deed, to Eddie's way of thinking. He wrote a letter to his wife, whom he hadn't seen for twelve years, and would have posted it if he could ever have found a stamp.

Occasionally he drifted back to the deck and got into a small game to keep his wrist limber and his head clear, but he didn't have to. Eddie had a roll. He didn't have to build up a bank in the preliminaries. He steered clear of spectacular play for two reasons. First, it was a waste of time. It was just as well to let the money get into a few hands before he exerted himself, and second, Eddie, at a time like this, preferred a kind of obscurity and anonymity. There was another reason too. The ship sailed on Tuesday and Eddie was waiting for Sunday, because he was particularly hot on Sundays, a fact he attributed to a clean and disinterested way of life. Once on a Sunday, and, understand, this is Mulligan's story, Eddie had won a small steam roller from a road gang in New Mexico, and on another Sunday Eddie had cleaned out a whole camp meeting, and in humility had devoted 10 per cent of his winnings to charity.

As the week went on the games began to fade out. There were fewer games and the stakes were larger. On Saturday there were only four good ones going, and at this time Eddie began to take interest. He played listlessly Saturday morning, but in the afternoon became more active and wiped out two of the games because his time was getting short and he didn't want too many games going the next day.

At ten o'clock the next day Eddie appeared on the deck, clean and combed and modest and bulging at the pockets of his field jacket. The game was going, but there were only three players in it. Eddie said innocently, "Mind if I get in for a pass or two?" The three players scrutinized him cynically. A Pole with one blue eye and one brown eye spoke roughly to him. "Froggy skins it takes, soldier," he said, "not is playing peanuts."

Eddie delicately exposed the butt end of a bank that looked like a rolled roast for a large supper. The Pole sighed with happiness, and the other two, who were remarkable and successful for no other reason than that they could disappear in a crowd, rubbed their hands involuntarily, as though to keep their fingers warm. Eddie concealed his poke as modestly as a young woman adjusts the straps of an evening gown that has no straps. He kneeled down beside the blanket and said, "What about is the tariff?" A wall of spectators closed behind him.

Eddie faded thirty of a hundred. The Pole rolled and won and let it lie, and Eddie took a hundred of the two hundred and the Pole shot a six and made it. Behind the dense circle of spectators running feet could be heard. This was to be a game. The ship took a slight list as GIs ran from all over just to be near a game like this, even if they couldn't see it.

The four hundred lay on the blanket like a large salad. The two disappearing men looked at Eddie, and Eddie went into his roll and undid four hundred in small bills and laid them timidly out. This Pole glared at him with his brown eye, and smiled at him with his blue eye, a trick which served him very well in poker, but had little effect on a crap game. He breathed on the dice and didn't speak to them. He rolled an eight and smiled with both his eyes. Again he breathed on the dice and cast them back-handed to show how easy that point was, and a four and a three looked up at him.

Eddie, breathing easily, relaxed and sure, pulled the big green salad gently to his side of the blanket. He unrolled two hundred more from his roll like toilet tissue, and laid them down. "One grand," he said, "all or part."

The Pole took half and the two anonymous men split up the rest, and Eddie rolled a rocking chair natural, a six and a five. "Leaving it lay," he said softly.

Only the Pole listened to him. He picked up the dice and looked them over carefully to be sure they were the ones he had put in himself. And then, scowling with both eyes, he covered Eddie. The pile of money was ten inches high now, and spilling down like a loose haycock.

Eddie hummed a little to himself as he rolled, and a seven settled firmly. The Pole snorted. Eddie said, "And leaving that lay, all or part, anybody." Breathing had stopped on the ship, only the engines went on. Mouths were open. Figures frozen in the dense crowd about the blanket. Only once in a while word was passed back about what was happening.

Scowling at Eddie, the Pole scraped bottom. A whole week of very tiring play for the Pole lay on the blanket, and the pot was set. Eddie was magnificent. He moved easily. He did not shake or rattle the dice or speak to them or beseech them. He simply rolled them out with childlike faith. For a long moment he stared uncomprehendingly at the snake eyes that stared back at him. And then his expression changed to one of horror. "No," he said, "somepins wrong. I win on Sunday, always win on Sunday."

A sergeant shuffled his feet uneasily. "Mister," he said. "Mister, you see, it ain't Sunday. We've went and crossed the date line. We lost Sunday."

Anyway, it's one of Mulligan's lies.

Africa

*   *

PLANE FOR AFRICA

A NORTH AFRICAN POST (*Via London*), *August 26, 1943*—At nine o'clock in the morning word comes that you have been accepted for Africa. You go to the office of the transportation officer. "Can you go tonight?" he asks. "Your baggage must be in at three. You will report to such and such an address at seven-thirty. Do not be late."

It is then about noon. You do the thousand things that are necessary for a shift of continents. You pack the one bag and store the other things which you will not take, the warm clothes and the papers and books. You call the people with whom you have made appointments and call them off.

At seven-thirty you arrive at the address given and from then on the process is out of your hands and it works very smoothly. At a quarter of eight you get in an Army truck and are taken to the station. An Army train is waiting. It is called a ghost train because it has no given destination. All kinds of units are getting on board the train: combat crews going out to get their ships, colonels who are going home after months in the field, couriers with bags and packages of mail. The combat crews carry pistols and knives and they have the huge bags of flying equipment with them. They are brown officers who have been serving in the desert and they look a little sick with fatigue.

A bomber crew that has not yet gone into action, indeed has not had a ship since it got overseas, has been working on English beer and has managed to get to the singing state. The whistle blows and everyone piles into the train. It is a sleeper.

There is no place to gather. You go to bed right away. In the corridor the singing crew leans out of the window and the men shriek at girls as the train starts. Then they break into "Home On the Range," but the noise of the train drowns them out. The beer was not strong enough to give them much of a lift. The blacked-out train roars through the night. The windows are shut and painted so that no light can shine out. The singing collapses and the crews retire to their staterooms.

At four-thirty in the morning the steward knocks on your door, sets a cup of tea on the little shelf over your bed, and leaves. You quickly drink the tea and shave in time to be out of the train at five. It is cold and rainy when you get out of the train. You don't know where you are. You were never told. Army trucks are waiting to take you to the airfield. Deep puddles of rain water are standing all about the little station. You climb into a truck and in a short while you have come to a huge airfield. This is one of the fields of Air Transport Command, which moves men and goods all over the world. Fighter planes are dispersed about the field, dimly visible through the rain. The C-54s stand ready to go.

This is a large and comfortable station. There are club-rooms and a bar and a large restaurant. It is cold outside and inside the fireplaces are piled high with glowing coals. In the largest clubroom are many people waiting their time to go. There are men who have been here a week and some crews which just got in. A phonograph is playing something sung by Dinah Shore. The men sleep on the couches and wait for their time.

The control-desk officer says, "Come back at one-thirty and you will be told when you go."

The nearest town is several miles away. The crews wander about for a while and then go back to the clubroom to read comic books—Superman and the rest. They read them without amusement, but with great concentration.

The officer says, "You will probably go in eight hours," and again the wandering. A ship is warming up. It is going home. The men on it will be in New York tomorrow. Even the ones who recently came over look longingly at these lucky ones. Just before they go they are cornered and messages given. "Call my wife and tell her that you saw me. Here is the telephone number." There would be letters to carry, but that is forbidden.

The men going home actually write the numbers down. They look a little self-conscious to be going home, and very happy about it, too. They get into the big ship and the door closes. It is a four-motored ship and you have to climb high to get into it. The little crowd stands in the entrance and watches it go and then it has disappeared into the rain almost before it is off the ground. The field has suddenly become very lonely. The men go back to the coal fires and to old copies of magazines, *Esquires* and *New Yorkers*, months old, copies of *Life* from April and May.

The officer says, "The plane will leave for Africa in fifteen minutes." It would seem the plane would be crowded, but it isn't. There are on board only one combat crew and two civilians. It is a C-54-A, which means that it has bucket seats and is more than half cargo plane. Now the crew are gathering together their bags and their parachutes, slinging on their pistols and knives and web equipment. They are being very nonchalant about the whole thing. Africa means nothing to them.

For a while we stand shivering in the rain while our names are called off. Then each one climbs the ladder and goes through the door. The windows of the plane are not blacked out, the way they are at home. They don't mind if you see. The big door slams, and outside you can hear the motors begin to turn over.

*   *

ALGIERS

ALGIERS (*Via London*), *August 28, 1943*—Algiers is a fantastic city now. Always a place of strange mixtures, it has been brought to a nightmarish mess by the influx of British and American troops and their equipment. Now jeeps and staff cars nudge their way among camels and horse-drawn cars.

The sunshine is blindingly white on the white city, and when there is no breeze from the sea the heat is intense.

The roads are lined with open wagons loaded high with fresh-picked grapes, with military convoys, with Arabs on horseback, with Canadians, Americans, Free French native troops in tall red hats. The uniforms are of all colors and all combinations of colors. Many of the French colonial troops have been issued American uniforms since they had none of their own. You never know when you approach American khaki that it will not clothe an Arab or a Senegalese.

The languages spoken in the streets are fascinating. Rarely is one whole conversation carried out in just one language. Our troops do not let language difficulties stand in their way. Thus you may see a soldier speaking in broad Georgia accents conversing with a Foreign Legionnaire and a burnoosed Arab. He speaks cracker, with a sour French word thrown in here and there, but his actual speech is with his hands. He acts out his conversation in detail.

His friends listen and watch and they answer him in Arabic or French and pantomime their meaning, and oddly enough they all understand one another. The spoken language is merely the tonal background to a fine bit of acting. Out of it comes a manual pidgin that is becoming formalized. The gesture for a drink is standard. Gestures of friendship and anger and love have also become standard.

The money is a definite problem. A franc is worth two cents. It is paper money and comes in five, ten, twenty, fifty, one hundred, and one thousand franc notes. The paper used is a kind of blotting paper that wads up and tears easily.

Carried in the pocket, it becomes wet and gummy with perspiration, and when taken out of the pocket often falls to pieces in your hands. In some stores they will not accept torn money, which limits the soldier, because most of the money he has is not only torn but wadded and used until the numbers on it are almost unrecognizable. A wad of money feels like a handful of warm wilted lettuce. In addition there are many American bills, the so-called invasion money, which is distinguished from home money by having a gold seal printed on its face. These bills feel cool and permanent compared with the Algerian money.

A whole new tourist traffic has set up here. A soldier may buy baskets, bad rugs, fans, paintings on cloth, just as he can at Coney Island. Many GIs with a magpie instinct will never be able to get home, such is their collection of loot. They have bits of battle debris, knives, pistols, bits of shell fragments, helmets, in addition to their colored baskets and rugs. In each case the collector has someone at home in mind when he makes the purchases. Grandma would love this Algerian shawl, and this Italian bayonet is just the thing to go over Uncle Charley's fireplace, along with the French bayonet he brought home from the last war. Suddenly there will come the order to march with light combat equipment, and the little masses of collections will have to be left with instructions to forward that will never be carried out. Americans are great collectors. The next station will start the same thing all over again.

The terraces of the hotels are crowded at five o'clock. This is the time when people gather to get a drink and to look at one another. There is no hard liquor. Cooled wine and lemonade and orange wine are the standard drinks. There is some beer made of peanuts, which does have a definite peanut flavor.

The wine is good and light and cooling, a little bit of a shock to a palate used to bourbon whisky, but acceptable.

On these terraces the soldiers come to sit about little tables and to meet dates. The French women here have done remarkably well. Their shoes have thick wooden soles, but are attractive, and the few clothes they have are clean and well kept. Since there is little material for dyeing the hair or bleaching it, a new fashion seems to have started. One lock of the hair is bleached and combed back over the unbleached part. It has a strange and not unattractive effect.

About five o'clock the streets are invaded by little black Wog boys with bundles of newspapers. They shriek, "*Stahs'n Straipes. Stahs'n Straipes.*" The Army newspaper is out again. This is the only news most of our men get. In fact, little news comes here. New York and London are much better informed than this station, which is fairly close to action. But it seems to be generally true that the closer to action you get, the more your interest in the over-all picture diminishes.

Soldiers here are not so much interested in the trend of war as the soldiers are in training camps at home. Here the qualities of the mess, the animosities with the sergeant, the price of wine are much more important than the world at war.

This is a mad, bright, dreamlike place. It is probable that our soldiers will remember it as a whirl of color and a polyglot babble. The heat makes your head a little vague, so that impressions run together and blot one another up. Outlines are hazy. It will be a curious memory when the soldiers try to sort it out to tell about after the war, and it will not be strange if they improvise a bit.

*   *

A WATCH CHISELER

A NORTH AFRICAN POST (*Via London*), *August 31, 1943*—It was well after midnight. The sergeant of MPs and his lieutenant drove in a jeep out of Sidi Belle Road from Oran. The sergeant had carved the handles of his gun from the Plexiglass from the nose of a bomber and he had begun to carve figures in it during off times with his pocket knife. It was a soft African night with abundant stars. The lieutenant was quite young and sensible enough to depend a good deal on his sergeant. The jeep leaped and rattled over cobblestones. "Let's go up to the Engineers and get a cup of coffee and a sandwich," the lieutenant said. "Turn around at the next corner."

At that moment a weapons carrier came roaring in from the country, going nearly sixty miles an hour. It flashed by the jeep and turned the corner on two wheels. "Jeezus," said the sergeant, "shall I go after him?"

"Run him down," said the lieutenant.

The sergeant wheeled the jeep around and put his foot to the floor. Around the corner he could see the tail lights in the distance and he seemed to gain on it rapidly. The weapons carrier was stopped, pulled up beside a field. The jeep skidded to a stop and the sergeant leaped out with the lieutenant after him.

Three men were sitting in the weapons carrier, three in the front seat. They were quite drunk. The sergeant flashed his light in the back. There were two empty wine bottles on the floor of the truck. "Get out," said the sergeant. As the men got out he frisked each one of them, tapping the hind pockets and the trousers below the knees. The three soldiers looked a little bedraggled.

"Who was driving that car?" the lieutenant asked.

"I don't know him," a small fat soldier said. "I never saw him before. He just jumped out and ran when he saw you coming. I never saw him before. We were just walking along and he asked us to come for a ride with him." The small fat soldier rushed the words out.

"That'll be enough out of you," the sergeant said. "You don't have to tell your friends the alibi. Where did you dump the stuff?"

"What stuff, Sergeant? I don't know what stuff you mean."

"You know what I mean all right. Shall I take a look about, sir?"

"Go ahead," the lieutenant said. The sergeant went to the border of the field and flashed his light about in the stubble. Then he came back. "Can't see anything," he said, and to the men, "Where'd you get this truck?"

"Just like I told you—this soldier asked us to come for a

ride, and then he saw you coming and he jumped out and ran."

"What was his name?"

"I don't know. We called him Willie. He said his name was Willie. I never saw him in my life before. Said his name was Willie."

"Get in the jeep," said the sergeant. "I've got the keys, lieutenant. We'll send out for the truck. Go on now, you guys, get in that jeep."

"We ain't done anything wrong, Sarge. What you going to take us in for? Guy named Willie just asked—"

"Shut up and get in," said the sergeant.

The three piled uncomfortably into the back seat of the jeep. The sergeant got behind the wheel and the lieutenant loosened his gun in its holster and sat on the little front seat with his body screwed around to face the three. Only the little man wanted to talk. The jeep rattled into the dark streets of Oran and pulled up in front of the M.P. station, jumped up on the sidewalk, and parked bumper against the building. Inside, brilliant lights were blinding after the blacked-out streets. A sergeant and a first lieutenant sat behind a big, high desk and looked over at the three ranged in front of them.

"Take off your dog tags and put them up here," said the sergeant. He began to make notes on a pad from the dog tags. "Put everything in your pockets in this box." He shoved a cigar box to the edge of the desk.

"But this here's my stuff," the little man protested.

"You'll get a receipt. Put it up and roll up your sleeves."

The two men who had been with the little fat man were silent and watchful. "Who was driving the truck?" the desk sergeant asked.

"A fellow named Willie. He jumped out and ran away."

The sergeant turned to the other two. "Who was driving the truck?" he asked them.

They both nodded their heads toward the little fat man and neither one of them spoke. "You bastards," the little fat man said quietly. "Oh, you dirty bastards."

"Roll up your sleeves," the desk sergeant said, and then: "Good God, four wrist watches. Say, this one is a GI watch. That's government property. Where did you get it?"

"I lent a fellow money for it. He's going to get it back when he pays me."

"Put your wallet up here."

The little fat man brought out a wallet of red morocco leather and hesitantly put it up. "I want a receipt for this. This is my savings."

The desk sergeant shook out the wallet. "God Almighty," he said, and he began to count the mounds of bills and he made notes on his pad. "Ten thousand Algerian francs and three thousand dollars, American," he said. "You really are packing the stuff away, aren't you, buddy?"

"That's my life savings," the little fat man said plaintively. "I want a receipt for that, that's my money."

The lieutenant behind the desk came to life. "Lock them up separately," he said. "I'll talk to them. Sergeant, you send a detail out for that truck and tell them to search the place all around there. Tell them to look out for watches, Elgins, GI watches. It will be a case about this size. It would have a thousand in it if they are all there. The Arabs are paying forty bucks for them. Okay, lock these men up."

"A guy named Willie," the fat man complained, "a guy

named Willie just asked us to come for a ride." He looked at the other two and his soft face was venomous. "Oh, you dirty bastards," he said.

*   *

OVER THE HILL

A NORTH AFRICAN POST (*Via London*), *September 1, 1943*—Sligo and the kid took their forty-eight-hour pass listlessly. The bars close in Algeria at eight o'clock but they got pretty drunk on wine before that happened and they took a bottle with them and lay down on the beach. The night was warm and after the two had finished the second bottle of wine they took off their clothes and waded out into the quiet water and then squatted down and sat there with only their heads out. "Pretty nice, eh, kid?" said Sligo. "There's guys used to pay heavy dough for stuff just like this and we get it for nothing."

"I'd rather be home on Tenth Avnoo," said the kid. "I'd rather be there than any place. I'd like to see my old lady. I'd like to see the World Series this year."

"You'd like maybe a clip in the kisser," said Sligo.

"I'd like to go into the Greek's and get me a double chocolate malted with six eggs in it," said the kid. He bobbed up to keep a little wavelet out of his mouth. "This place is lonely. I like Coney."

"Too full of people," said Sligo.

"This place is lonely," said the kid.

"Talking about the Series, I'd like to do that myself," said Sligo. "It's just times like this a fella gets kind of tempted to go over the hill."

"S'posen you went over the hill—where the hell would you go? There ain't no place to go."

"I'd go home," said Sligo. "I'd go to the Series. I'd be first in the bleachers, like I was in 'forty."

"You couldn't get home," the kid said; "there ain't no way to get home."

The wine was warming Sligo and the water was good. "I got dough says I can get home," he said carelessly.

"How much dough?"

"Twenty bucks."

"You can't do it," said the kid.

"You want to take the bet?"

"Sure, I'll take it. When you going to pay?"

"I ain't going to pay, you're going to pay. Let's go up on the beach and knock off a little sleep." . . .

At the piers the ships lay. They had brought landing craft and tanks and troops and now they lay, taking in the scrap, the broken equipment from the North African battlefields which would go to the blast furnaces to make more tanks and landing craft. Sligo and the kid sat on a pile of C-ration boxes and watched the ships. Down the hill came a detail with a hundred Italian prisoners to be shipped to New York. Some of the prisoners were ragged and some were dressed in American khaki because they had been too ragged in the wrong places. None of the prisoners seemed to be unhappy about going to America. They marched down to a gangplank and then stood in a crowd, awaiting orders to get aboard.

"Look at them," said the kid, "they get to go home and we got to stay. What you doing, Sligo? What you rubbing oil all over your pants for?"

"Twenty bucks," said Sligo, "and I'll find you and collect, too." He stood off and took off his overseas cap and tossed it to the kid. "Here's a present, kid."

"What you going to do, Sligo?"

"Don't you come follow me, you're too dumb. Twenty bucks, and don't you forget it. So long, see you on Tenth Avnoo."

The kid watched him go, uncomprehending. Sligo, with dirty pants and a ripped shirt, moved gradually over, near to the prisoners, and then imperceptibly he edged in among them and stood bareheaded, looking back at the kid.

An order was called down to the guards, and they herded the prisoners toward the gangplank. Sligo's voice came plaintively. "I'm not supposed to be here. Hey, don't put me on dis ship."

"Shut up, wop," a guard growled at him. "I don't care if you did live sixteen years in Brooklyn. Git up that plank." He pushed the reluctant Sligo up the gangplank.

Back on the pile of boxes the kid watched with admiration. He saw Sligo get to the rail. He saw Sligo still protesting and fighting to get back to the pier. He heard him shrieking, "Hey, I'm Americano, Americano soldier. You canna poot me here."

The kid saw Sligo struggling and then he saw the final triumph. He saw Sligo take a sock at a guard and he saw the guard's club rise and come down on Sligo's head. His friend collapsed and was carried out of sight on board the ship. "The son of a gun," the kid murmured to himself. "The smart son of a gun. They can't do nothing at all to him and he got witnesses. Well, the smart son of a gun. My God, it's worth twenty bucks."

The kid sat on the boxes for a long time. He didn't leave his place till the ship cast off and the tugs pulled her clear of the submarine nets. The kid saw the ship join the group and he saw the destroyers move up and take the convoy under protection. The kid walked dejectedly up to the town. He bought a bottle of Algerian wine and headed back toward the beach to sleep his forty-eight.

*   *

THE SHORT SNORTER WAR MENACE

SOMEWHERE IN AFRICA (*Via London*), *September 2, 1943*—The growth of the Short Snorters is one of the greatest single menaces to come out of the war so far. The idea started as a kind of joke in a time when very few people flew over an ocean in an airplane. It became the custom then for the crew of the airplane to sign their names on a one-dollar bill which made the new ocean flyer a Short Snorter. He was supposed to keep this bill always with him. If at any time he were asked if he were a Short Snorter and he did not have his signed bill with him he was forced to pay a dollar to each member present at the time when the question was asked. It was good fun and a kind of general joke and also it was a means of getting someone to pay for the drinks.

But then came the war and the building of thousands of ships and the transporting of thousands of men overseas by airplane and every single one becomes a Short Snorter. There are hundreds of thousands of Short Snorters now who have actually flown over an ocean and there are further hundreds of thousands who carry signed bills. And the new Short Snorter goes much farther than having his bill signed by the crew which carried him on his initial crossing. The custom has grown to have the bill signed by everyone you come across. At a bar you ask your drinking companion to sign your bill. You ask generals and actors and senators to sign your bill.

With the growing autographing one bill soon was not enough. You procured another bill and stuck it with Scotch tape to your first bill. Then the thing went farther. You began to collect bills from other countries. To your American dollar bill you stuck a one-pound English note, and to it a fifty-franc Algerian note, and to it a hundred-lira bill. Every place you went you stuck the money to your growing Short Snorter until now there are people who have streamers eight and ten feet long, which, folded and rolled, make a great bundle in the pocket, and these streamers are covered with thousands of names and represent besides considerable money. Even the one-dollar original is disappearing. Many new Short Snorters use $20 bills and some even $100 bills.

These are the new autograph books. The original half of

the joke has been lost. In bars, in airports, in clubs, the first thing that must be done is a kind of general exchange of signatures. Serious and intelligent gentlemen sign one another's bills with an absolute lack of humor. If the party is fairly large it might take an hour before everyone has signed the bill of everyone else. Meanwhile the soup gets cold.

There are favorite places on the bill for honored and desirable autographs. The little space under Morgenthau's name is one such. The wide space beside the portrait on the bill is another. If you get an autograph you want to show, you have it written on a clear space, but if it is just one of the run-of-the-mill signatures it is put any place in the green part, where it hardly shows up at all. It is a frantic, serious-minded, insane thing. Men of dignity scramble for autographs on their Short Snorters. A special case, usually made of cellophane, is sometimes carried to house the bill, or the long streamers of bills, because these treasures are handled so much that they would fall to pieces if they were not protected.

The effort and time involved in this curious thing is immense. Entertainers who travel about to our troops sign literally thousands of Short Snorter bills. For no longer do people have to fly an ocean to be members. The new method is that any Short Snorter can create a new Short Snorter. The club is pyramiding. Probably there are ten million Short Snorters now and every day new thousands begin to scribble on their bills. It would be interesting to know how many bills are withdrawn from circulation to be used as autograph books. They must run into the millions.

The use of large bills as Short Snorter bills has a curious logic behind it. The man or woman who used a $20 or $100 bill feels that he or she will not spend this money because of the signatures on it, but he also feels that if he needs to he can spend it. Thus he has a nest egg or mad money and a treasure, too. He will not toss it over a bar nor put it in a crap game, but if he really should get into a hole he has this money with him.

Very curious practices grow out of a war and surely none more strange than this one has taken over the public recently.

*   *

THE BONE YARD

A NORTH AFRICAN POST (*Via London*), *September 5, 1943*—On the edge of a North African city there is a huge used tank yard. It isn't only tanks, either. It is a giant bone yard, where wrecked tanks and trucks and artillery are brought and parked, ready for overhauling. There are General Shermans with knocked-out turrets and broken tracks, with engines gone to pieces. There are trucks that have fallen into shell holes. There are hundreds of wrecked motorcycles and many broken and burned-out pieces of artillery, the debris of months of bitter fighting in the desert.

On the edge of this great bone yard are the reconditioning

yards and the rebuilding lines. Into the masses of wrecked equipment the Army inspectors go. They look over each piece of equipment and tag it. Perhaps this tank, with a German .88 hole drilled neatly through the turret, will go into the fight again with a turret from the one next to it, which has had the tracks shot from under it. Most of the tanks will run again, but those which are beyond repair will furnish thousands of spare parts to take care of the ones which are running. This plant is like the used-car lots in American cities, where you can, for a small price, buy the gear or the wheel which keeps your car running.

The engines are removed from the wrecked trucks and put on the repair lines. Here a complete overhaul job is done, the linings of the motors rebored, with new rings, tested and ready to go finally into the paint room, where they are resprayed with green paint. Housings, gears, clutch plates are cleaned with steam, inspected, and placed in bins, ready to be drawn again as spare parts. One whole end of the yard is piled high with repaired tires. Hundreds of men work in this yard, putting the wrecked equipment back to work.

Here is an acre of injured small artillery, 20- and 37-mm. anti-tank guns. Some of them have been fired so long that their barrels have burned out. Some of them have only a burst tire or a bent trail. These are sorted and put ready for repair. The barrels are changed for new ones, and the old ones go to the scrap pile. For when everything usable has been made use of there is still a great pile of twisted steel which can be used as nothing but scrap metal. But the ships which bring supplies to the Army from home are going back. They take their holds full of this scrap to go into the making of new steel for new equipment.

It is interesting to see the same American who, a few months ago, was tinkering with engines in a small-town garage now tinkering with the engine of a General Grant tank. And the man hasn't changed a bit. He is still the intent man who is good with engines. He isn't even dressed very much differently, for the denim work clothes are very like the overalls he has been wearing for years. Beside these men work the French and the Arabs. They are learning from our men how to take care of the machinery that they may use. They learn quickly but without many words, for most of our men cannot speak the language of the men who are helping them. It is training by sign language and it seems to work very well.

The wrecked equipment comes in in streams from the battlefields. Modern war is very hard on its tools. While in this war fewer men are killed, more equipment than ever is wrecked, for it seems almost to be weapon against weapon rather than man against man.

But there are many sad little evidences in the vehicles. In this tank which has been hit there is a splash of blood against the steel side of the turret. And in this burned-out tank a large piece of singed cloth and a charred and curled shoe. And the insides of a tank are full of evidences of the men who ran it, penciled notes written on the walls, a telephone number, a sketch of a profile on the steel armor plate. Probably every vehicle in the whole Army has a name, usually the name of a girl but sometimes a brave name like Hun Chaser. That one got badly hit. And there is a tank with no track and with the whole top of the turret shot away by a heavy shell, but on her skirt in front is still her name and she is called *Lucky Girl*. Every one of these vehicles lying in the wreck yard has some tremendous story, but in many of the cases the story died with the driver and the crew.

There are little tags tied to the barrels of the guns. One says: "The recoil slaps sideways. I'm scared of it." And another says: "You can't hit a barn with this any more." And in a little while these guns, refitted and painted, with their camouflage, will be back in the fight again.

There is hammering in the yard, and fizz of welders and hiss of steam pipes. The men are stripped to the waist, working under the hot African sun, their skins burned nearly black. The little cranes run excitedly about, carrying parts, stacking engines, tearing the hopeless jobs to pieces for their usable parts.

Italy

*   *

REHEARSAL

SOMEWHERE IN MEDITERRANEAN WAR THEATER, *September 29, 1943*—American troops trained on the beaches of North Africa for the beaches of Italy. It was hot and dusty on the land, and back from the coast there were many training props for them to work with. There were wooden landing barges standing on the ground in which dusty men crouched, until at a signal the ramp went down and they charged out and took cover. To get ashore quickly, and to get down behind some hummock of earth where the machine guns can't get at you, is very important stuff in landing.

And so they practiced over and over, and instead of getting wet they only raised clouds of dust, the light, reddish dust of Africa, in colors little like the red soil of Georgia.

And when the men had learned to leap out and charge and take cover and to run forward again, presenting as little of themselves as possible to the observing officers, they went to the set to learn how to conduct themselves on entering an enemy town.

There were sets like those in a Hollywood studio in the old silent days, wooden fronts and tall and short buildings with open windows and little streets between, and there the men learned how to crouch on a corner and how to slink under the cover of walls. They learned with practice grenades how to blast out a machine gun set up in a building. It was strange to see them rehearsing, as though for a play. It went on for weeks.

And when they had become used to the method and when they reacted almost instinctively, they were taken finally to the Mediterranean beaches, the long, white beaches, which are not very unlike the beaches at Salerno. The water is incredibly blue there and the beaches are white. And the water is very salty. You float like a cork on it. On the beaches they practiced with real landing barges. The teams put out to sea and then turned and made runs for the shore and the iron ramps clattered down and the men rushed ashore and crept and wriggled their way up to the line of the shore where the grapevines began, for there are vineyards in Italy, too.

When they had practiced a little while, machine guns with live ammunition fired over their heads, but not very far over their heads, to give them a real interest in keeping low.

Now in larger groups they rushed in from the sea and charged up into the vines and crept up through the vineyards and moved inland. An amazing number of men can disappear into a vineyard so that you can't see them at all.

The dark Algerian grapes were ripe and as they crawled the men picked the grapes and ate them and the incidence of GI dysentery skyrocketed, but there is no way of keeping a dusty, thirsty man from eating ripe grapes, particularly if they are hanging right over his head, when he lies under the vines.

Over and over again they captured this little sector and climbed up and captured the heights. They had to learn to do it in the daytime because when they would really do it it would be in the dark of the early morning. But when the training for each day was finished, the men went back to the beaches and took off their clothes and played in the water. The water was warm and delightful and the salt stung their eyes. Their bodies grew browner day by day until they were only a little lighter than the Arabs.

At night they were very tired and there is not much to do in Africa after dark anyway. No love is lost for the Arabs. They are the dirtiest people in the world and among the smelliest. The whole countryside smells of urine, four thousand years of urine. That is the characteristic smell of North Africa. The men were not allowed to go into the native cities because there was a great deal of disease and besides there are too many little religious rules and prejudices that an unsuspecting dogface can run afoul of. And there wasn't much to buy and what there was cost too much. The prices have skyrocketed on the coming of the troops.

The men slept in their pup tents and drew their mosquito nets over them and scratched and cursed all night until, after a time, they were too tired to scratch and curse and they fell asleep the moment they hit the blankets. Their minds and their bodies became machine-like. They did not talk about the war. They talked only of home and of clean beds with white sheets and they talked of ice water and ice cream and places that did not smell of urine. Most of them let their minds dwell on snow banks and the sharp winds of Middle Western winter. But the red dust blew over them and crusted their skins and after a while they could not wash it all off any more. The war had narrowed down to their own small group of men and their own job. It would be a lie to suggest that they like being there. They wish they were somewhere else.

*   *

SOMEWHERE IN THE MEDITERRANEAN WAR THEATER, *October 1, 1943*—Week after week the practice of the invasion continued, gathering impetus as the day grew nearer. Landing operations and penetrations, stealthy approaches and quick charges. The whole thing gradually took on increased speed as the day approached.

The roads back of the coast were crowded with staff cars dashing about. The highways were lined with trucks full of the incredible variety of war material for the invasion of Italy. There are thousands of items necessary to a modern army and, because of the complexity of supply, a modern army is a sluggish thing. Plans, once made, are not easily changed, for every move of combat troops is paralleled by hundreds of moves behind the lines, the moves of food and ammunition, trucks that must get there on time. If the whole big, sluggish animal does not move with perfect co-operation, it is very likely that it will not move at all. Modern warfare is very like an automobile assembly line. If one bolt in the whole machine is out of place or not available, the line must stop and wait for it. Improvisation is not very possible.

And all over in the practice zones in North Africa the practice went on to make sure that every bolt would be in its place. The men went on field rations to get used to them. Canteens must always be full, but full of the evil-tasting, disinfected water which gets your mouth wet but gives you very little other pleasure.

While the men went through their final training on the beaches the implements of war were collecting for their use. In huge harbors, whose names must not be mentioned, transports and landing craft of all kinds were accumulating. They crept up to the piers and opened the doors in their noses and took on their bellyfuls of tanks and loaded trucks and then slipped out and sat at anchor and waited for the "D" day at the "H" hour, which very few in the whole Army knew.

On the freighters cranes slung full-loaded trucks and laden two-and-a-half-ton "ducks," which are perhaps America's real secret weapon of this war. The "ducks," big trucks which lumber down the beaches and enter the water and become boats, or the boats which, coming loaded to the beach, climb out, and drive as trucks along the dusty roads.

In the harbors the accumulations of waiting ships collected, tank-landing craft and troop-landing craft of all kinds. The barges, which run up on the beaches and disgorge their loads and back off and go for more. And on the piers

Arab workers passed the hundreds of thousands of cases of canned rations to the lighters and the lighters moved out and filled the ships with food for the soldiers. The fleets accumulated until they choked the harbor.

Now the enemy knew what was going on. They had to know. The operation was too great for them not to know. They sent their planes over the harbor to try to bomb the gathering fleets and they were driven off and destroyed by the protecting Beaufighters and P-38s. They did not succeed in doing damage, for finally the enemy had lost control of the skies and the fleets could load at least in peace.

But at night they tried to get through and the flak rose up at them, like all the Fourth of Julys in history, the ships and the shore batteries put up a wall of fire against the invading planes so that some of them unloaded their bombs in the open countryside and some of them exploded with their own bombs and some went crashing into the sea. But they had lost control.

Now "D" day was coming close and at headquarters the officers collected and held conference after conference and there was a growing tautness in the whole organization. Staff officers dashed in to their briefs and rushed back to their units to brief those under them. It would have been easy to know how close the time had come by the tempo, and then suddenly it was all done and a curious quiet settled on the whole invasion force.

Somewhere an order passed and in the night the ships began to move out to the places of rendezvous. And in the night the columns of men climbed into trucks and the trucks came down the piers to the ships, and the men, like ants, crawled on the ships and sat down on their equipment. And the troopships slipped out to the rendezvous to wait for the moment to leave.

It was no start with bugles and flags or cheering men. The radios crackled their coded orders. Messages went from radio rooms to the bridges of the ships. The word was passed to the engine rooms and the great convoys put out to sea.

And on the decks of troopships and on the flat iron floors of the landing craft, the men sat on their lumpy mountains of equipment and waited. The truck drivers sat in their trucks on the ships and waited. The tank men stayed close to their iron monsters and waited. The ships moved out into their formations and the destroyers came tearing in and took up their places on the flanks and before and after the ships. Out of sight, in all directions, the fighting ships combed the ocean for submarines and the listening devices strained for the signal which means a steel enemy is creeping near.

Over the convoy the silver balloons hung in the southern sunlight, balloons to keep the dive-bombers off. And then the sun went down. The balloons kept the sun for half an hour after it had gone from the surface of the sea. There was radio silence now and the darkness came down and the great convoy crept on toward Italy. The sea was smooth and only the weakest stomachs were bothered.

There were no lights showing, but a pale moon lighted the dark ships somberly and the slow wakes disturbed the path of the moon on the ocean.

The combat troops sat on the luggage and waited. This was what it was all for. They had left home for this. They had studied and trained, changed their natures and their clothing and their habits all toward this time. And still there were only a very few men who knew "D" day and "H" hour.

*   *

INVASION

SOMEWHERE IN THE MEDITERRANEAN THEATER, *October 3, 1943*—On the iron floors of the LCIs, which stands for Landing Craft Infantry, the men sit about and for a time they talk and laugh and make jokes to cover the great occasion. They try to reduce this great occasion to something normal, something ordinary, something they are used to. They rag one another, accuse one another of being scared, they repeat experiences of recent days, and then gradually silence creeps over them and they sit silently because the hugeness of the experience has taken them over.

These are green troops. They have been trained to a fine point, hardened and instructed, and they lack only one thing to make them soldiers, enemy fire, and they will never be soldiers until they have it. No one, least of all themselves, knows what they will do when the terrible thing happens. No man there knows whether he can take it, knows whether he will run away or stick, or lose his nerve and go to pieces, or will be a good soldier. There is no way of knowing and probably that one thing bothers you more than anything else.

And that is the difference between green troops and soldiers. Tomorrow at this time these men, those who are living, will be different. They will know then what they can't know tonight. They will know how they face fire. Actually there is little danger. They are going to be good soldiers, for they do not know that this is the night before the assault. There is no way for any man to know it.

In the moonlight on the iron deck they look at each other strangely. Men they have known well and soldiered with are strange and every man is cut off from every other one, and in their minds they search the faces of their friends for the dead. Who will be alive tomorrow night? I will, for one. No one ever gets killed in the war. Couldn't possibly. There would be no war if anyone got killed. But each man, in this last night in the moonlight, looks strangely at the others and sees death there. This is the most terrible time of all. This night before the assault by the new green troops. They will never be like this again.

Every man builds in his mind what it will be like, but it is never what he thought it would be. When he designs the assault in his mind he is alone and cut off from everyone. He is alone in the moonlight and the crowded men about him are strangers in this time. It will not be like this. The fire and the movement and the exertion will make him a part of these strangers sitting about him, and they will be a part of him, but he does not know that now. This is a bad time, never to be repeated.

Not one of these men is to be killed. That is impossible, and it is no contradiction that every one of them is to be killed. Every one is in a way dead already. And nearly every man has written his letter and left it somewhere to be posted if he is killed. The letters, some misspelled, some illiterate, some polished and full of attitudes, and some meager and tight. All say the same thing. They all say: "I wish I had told you, and I never did, I never could. Some obscure and impish thing kept me from ever telling you, and only now, when it is too late, can I tell you. I've thought these things," the letters say, "but when I started to speak something cut me off. Now I can say it, but don't let it be a burden on you. I just know that it was always so, only I didn't say it." In every letter that is the message. The piled-up reticences go down in the last letters. The letters to wives, and mothers, and sisters, and fathers, and, such is the hunger to have been a part of someone, letters sometimes to comparative strangers.

The great ships move through the night though they are covered now, and the engines make no noise. Orders are given in soft voices and the conversation is quiet. Somewhere up ahead the enemy is waiting and he is silent too. Does he know we are coming, and does he know when and in what number? Is he lying low with his machine guns ready and his mortars set on the beaches, and his artillery in the hills? What is he thinking now? Is he afraid or confident?

The officers know H-hour now. The moon is going down. H-hour is 3:30, just after the moon has set and the shore is black. The convoy is to moonward of the shore. Perhaps with glasses the enemy can see the convoy against the setting moon, but ahead where we are going there is only a misty pearl-like grayness. The moon goes down into the ocean and ships that have been beside you and all around you disappear into the blackness and only the tiny shielded position-lights show where they are.

The men sitting on the deck disappear into the blackness and the silence, and one man begins to whistle softly just to be sure he is there.

*   *

SOMEWHERE IN THE MEDITERRANEAN THEATER, *October 4, 1943*—There is a good beach at Salerno, and a very good landing at Red Beach No. 2. The ducks were coming loaded ashore and running up out of the water and joining the lines of trucks, and the pontoon piers were out in the water with large landing cars up against them. Along the beach the bulldozers were at work pushing up sand ramps for the trucks to land on and just back of the beach were the white tapes that mean land mines have not been cleared out.

There are little bushes on the sand dunes at Red Beach, south of the Sele River, and in a hole in the sand buttressed by sandbags a soldier sat with a leather-covered steel telephone beside him. His shirt was off and his back was dark with sunburn. His helmet lay in the bottom of the hole and his rifle was on a little pile of brush to keep sand out of it. He had staked a shelter half on a pole to shade him from the sun, and he had spread bushes on top of that to camouflage it. Beside him was a water can and an empty C-ration can to drink out of.

The soldier said, "Sure you can have a drink. Here, I'll pour it for you." He tilted the water can over the tin cup. "I hate to tell you what it tastes like," he said.

I took a drink. "Well, doesn't it?" he said.

"It sure does," I said.

Up in the hills the .88s were popping and the little bursts threw sand about. His face was streaked where the sweat had run down through the dirt, and his hair and his eyebrows were sunburned almost white. But there was a kind of gaiety about him. His telephone buzzed and he answered it and said, "Hasn't come through yet, sir, no sir I'll tell him." He clicked off the phone.

"When'd you come ashore?" he asked. And then, without waiting for an answer, he went on. "I came in just before dawn yesterday. I wasn't with the very first, but right in the second." He seemed to be very glad about it. "It was hell," he said, "it was bloody hell." He seemed to be gratified at the hell it was, and that was right. The great question had been solved for him. He had been under fire. He knew now what he would do under fire. He would never have to go through that uncertainty again. "I got pretty near up to there," he said, and pointed to two beautiful Greek temples about a mile away. "And then I got sent back here for beach communications. When did you say you got ashore?" And again he didn't wait for an answer.

"It was dark as hell," he said, "and we were just waiting out there." He pointed to the sea where the mass of the invasion fleet rested. "If we thought we were going to sneak ashore we were nuts," he said. "They were waiting for us. They knew just where we were going to land. They had machine guns in the sand dunes and .88s on the hills.

"We were out there all packed in an LCI, and then all hell broke loose. The sky was full of it and the star shells lighted it up and the tracers crisscrossed and the noise—we saw the assault go in, and then one of them hit a surf mine and went up, and in the light you could see them go flying about. I could see the boats land and the guys go wiggling and running, and then maybe there'd be a lot of white lines and some of them would waddle about and collapse and some would hit the beach.

"It didn't seem like men getting killed, more like a picture, like a moving picture. We were pretty crowded up in there, though, and then all of a sudden it came on me that this wasn't a moving picture. Those were guys getting the hell shot out of them, and then I got kind of scared, but what I wanted to do mostly was move around. I didn't like being cooped up there where you couldn't get away or get down close to the ground.

"Well, the firing would stop and then it would get pitch black even then, and it was just beginning to get light too, but the .88s sort of winked on the hills like messages, and the shells were bursting all around us. They had lots of .88s and they shot at everything. I was just getting real scared when we got the order to move in, and I swear that is the longest trip I ever took, that mile to the beach. I thought we'd never get there. I figured that if I was only on the beach I could dig down and get out of the way. There was too damned many of us there in that LCI. I wanted to spread out. That one that hit the mine was still burning when we went on by it. Then we bumped the beach and the ramps went down and I hit the water up to my waist.

"The minute I was on the beach I felt better. It didn't seem like everybody was shooting at me and I got up to that line of brush and flopped down and some other guys flopped down beside me and then we got feeling a little foolish. We stood up and moved on. Didn't say anything to each other, we just moved on. It was coming daylight then and the flashes of the guns weren't so bright. I felt a little like I was drunk. The ground heaved around under my feet and I was dull. I guess that was because of the firing. My ears aren't so good yet. I guess we moved up too far because I got sent back here." He laughed openly. "I might have gone on right into Rome if someone hadn't sent me back. I guess I might have walked right up that hill there."

The cruisers began firing on the hill and the .88s fired back. From over near the hill came the heavy thudding of .50-caliber machine guns. The soldier felt pretty good. He knew what he could do now. He said, "When did you say you came ashore?"

*   *

MEDITERRANEAN THEATER, *October 6, 1943*—You can't see much of a battle. Those paintings reproduced in history books which show long lines of advancing troops are either idealized or else times and battles have changed. The account in the morning papers of the battle of yesterday was not seen by the correspondent, but was put together from reports.

What the correspondent really saw was dust and the nasty burst of shells, low bushes and slit trenches. He lay on his stomach, if he had any sense, and watched ants crawling among the little sticks on the sand dune, and his nose was so close to the ants that their progress was interfered with by it.

Then he saw an advance. Not straight lines of men marching into cannon fire, but little groups scuttling like crabs from bits of cover to other cover, while the high chatter of machine guns sounded, and the deep proom of shellfire.

Perhaps the correspondent scuttled with them and hit

the ground again. His report will be of battle plan and tactics, of taken ground or lost terrain, of attack and counterattack. But these are some of the things he probably really saw:

He might have seen the splash of dirt and dust that is a shell burst, and a small Italian girl in the street with her stomach blown out, and he might have seen an American soldier standing over a twitching body, crying. He probably saw many dead mules, lying on their sides, reduced to pulp. He saw the wreckage of houses, with torn beds hanging like shreds out of the spilled hole in a plaster wall. There were red carts and the stalled vehicles of refugees who did not get away.

The stretcher-bearers come back from the lines, walking in off step, so that the burden will not be jounced too much, and the blood dripping from the canvas, brother and enemy in the stretchers, so long as they are hurt. And the walking wounded coming back with shattered arms and bandaged heads, the walking wounded struggling painfully to the rear.

He would have smelled the sharp cordite in the air and the hot reek of blood if the going has been rough. The burning odor of dust will be in his nose and the stench of men and animals killed yesterday and the day before. Then a whole building is blown up and an earthy, sour smell comes from its walls. He will smell his own sweat and the accumulated sweat of an army. When his throat is dry he will drink the warm water from his canteen, which tastes of disinfectant.

While the correspondent is writing for you of advances and retreats, his skin will be raw from the woolen clothes he has not taken off for three days, and his feet will be hot and dirty and swollen from not having taken off his shoes for days. He will itch from last night's mosquito bites and from today's sand-fly bites. Perhaps he will have a little sand-fly fever, so that his head pulses and a red rim comes into his vision. His head may ache from the heat and his eyes burn with the dust. The knee that was sprained when he leaped ashore will grow stiff and painful, but it is no wound and cannot be treated.

"The 5th Army advanced two kilometers," he will write, while the lines of trucks churn the road to deep dust and truck drivers hunch over their wheels. And off to the right the burial squads are scooping slits in the sandy earth. Their charges lie huddled on the ground and before they are laid in the sand, the second of the two dog tags is detached so that you know that that man with that Army serial number is dead and out of it.

These are the things he sees while he writes of tactics and strategy and names generals and in print decorates heroes. He takes a heavily waxed box from his pocket. That is his dinner. Inside there are two little packets of hard cake which have the flavor of dog biscuits. There is a tin can of cheese and a roll of vitamin-charged candy, an envelope of lemon powder to make the canteen water taste less bad, and a tiny package of four cigarettes.

That is dinner, and it will keep him moving for several more hours and keep his stomach working and his heart pumping. And if the line has advanced beyond him while he eats, dirty, buglike children will sidle up to him, cringing and sniffling, their noses ringed with flies, and these children will whine for one of the hard biscuits and some of the vitamin candy. They will cry for candy: "*Caramela—caramela—cara-*

mela—okay, okay, shank you, good-by." And if he gives the candy to one, the ground will spew up more dirty, buglike children, and they will scream shrilly, *"Caramela—caramela."* The correspondent will get the communiqué and will write your morning dispatch on his creaking, dust-filled portable: "General Clark's 5th Army advanced two kilometers against heavy artillery fire yesterday."

*   *

SOMEWHERE IN THE MEDITERRANEAN WAR THEATER, *October 8, 1943*—The invasion and taking of the beachhead at Salerno has been very rough. The German was waiting for us. His .88s were on the surrounding hills and his machine guns in the sand dunes. His mines were in the surf and he sat there and waited for us. There was no other way. He had to be pushed out. And, for a time, it looked as though we might be pushed out. But gradually, what with the naval ships firing and the determined holding out of recently green troops and the coming of our reserves from the sea, the picture has changed. Now the invasion fleet lies in comparative safety off the shore and the beach is secure.

The sea has been smooth during the whole thing. Any

storm would have made it more difficult, but the sea has been kind to us. It is as slick as silk and littered for many miles with little twinkling C-ration cans floating in the sea and glittering under the sun. The water is oily, too, and there are bits of wreckage floating everywhere and all the garbage of this huge fleet, the crates and cans and bottles and debris that men have the ability to scatter about.

Near shore the cruisers and battleships continue to fire, but now their guns are elevated and they fire over the mountains at targets unseen from the sea.

The command ship lies protected in the middle of the invasion fleet. She is a floating radio station. From her all the orders have gone out and to her all the news has come in. And the staffs are brutally tired. This has not been the usual thing. The command ship has been bombed at constantly. Her crew has been alerted every half-hour in the twenty-four. The bugle is blown and then the boatswain's pipe over the loudspeaker and then the crackling horn that means battle stations. Then tired staff officers have taken off their helmets and their lifebelts and made for the deck for their assigned stations, while the anti-aircraft roared over their heads and the bombs came down and burst the water into the air.

Not many German planes have got through the air cover, but some have and nearly every one was after the command ship. They have straddled her with bombs. There have been near misses that jerked her in the water and it is a wonder her plates aren't sprung.

And this has been going on for four days. No one has had any sleep. What has made it even worse, the Jerry planes have been talking to each other on their radios and not bothering to code their messages. They have been looking for this particular ship and aiming for her. They know that if they get this ship they may get the controlling brains of the whole operation.

There are very tired colonels and generals on board, waiting for the order to go ashore and establish headquarters. They will feel much better when they are ashore. It is not nice to be aboard the target of the whole fleet. But the command ship has not been hit. Other ships about her have been blasted, but not the command. The feeling aboard has been that the luck is getting pretty thin and that the next one must get her.

Meanwhile, the litter spreads out to sea on little currents. There will be C-ration cans come ashore for a thousand miles. The litter will coat the shores of Italy.

What has made the command ship's life even more lively is that the Germans have a new bomb. At least, that is the rumor. This bomb is released and then controlled from the plane. It is directed by radio, and if it seems about to miss it can be turned by its master. At least that is what is said. And surely these bombs do not seem to act like other ones. They come down more slowly, and they glow as they come, with something like a phosphorescence that you can even see in the daytime.

When the red signal for an air attack goes out, the destroyers move in circles, belching smoke, and the small smoke carriers dart busily among the big ships, trailing ribbons of white, choking smoke which smells like sulphur. The little boats weave in and out, until they have covered the fleet with their artificial fog. The sound of coughing is deafening. At least it is until the anti-aircraft starts. And then, through the smoke, you hear the deep blow of the bombs. They don't sound like anything else. And their explosions come through the water and strike the ship. You can feel them in your feet.

The endless lines of landing craft go ashore, carrying the supplies for men who are lying off in the bushes on the forward lines. Cases of food and tons of shells and cartridges. A hell of them lines the shore, waiting to be transported inland.

And the battle line has moved up. The beach is taken now and the invasion moves ahead. The white hospital ships move inshore to take on their cargoes.

*   *

PALERMO

SOMEWHERE IN THE MEDITERRANEAN THEATER, *October 11, 1943*—The sea off Sicily was running in long, smooth waves without whitecaps and the day was bright and the sea that Mediterranean blue that is unlike any other blue in the world. The PT boat ground its way through, making a great churned wake and taking even what little sea there was over the bow. It's the wettest boat of all, the torpedo boat. The crew, in their rubber clothes, huddled on the deck trying to keep out of the constant spray, and on each side of the bridge the machine-gunners, at their stations, sat in their turrets behind their guns and the water glistened on their faces. The cartridge cases of the .50-caliber shells were green from contact with the sea water.

Off to the right a body was floating in the sea, rising and falling on the long waves. It was pretty swollen, and the brown lifebelt and collar made it float high in the water.

The captain was dressed in a bathing suit and he was barefooted. The First had a rubber coat on but his trousers were rolled up and his feet were bare, too. The two of them looked off across the port torpedo tube at the floating body.

"Should we go over and take a look?" the First said.

"Not in the shape it's in," the captain said. "Besides, we have to make our schedule."

The First said, "I think that's the loneliest thing in the world. A body floating at sea. I don't know anything that looks so alone."

The captain let go his hold on the torpedo tube and turned and held onto the rail behind the port gun turret. "Before you came on I had one that gave me the willies," he said. He broke abruptly into his story.

"After Palermo fell," he said, "there was a night and a part of a day before the Seventh Army got to the city. I was on patrol with five PTs and we got the flash and we were in the neighborhood anyway, so we came to take a look. You know what Palermo looks like. That great, big, strong mountain right beside the city and the crazy lights that get on it and then the city spilled down there at the base. It looks like Ulysses has just left there. You can really get the sense of Vergil from that mountain, from the whole northern coast of Sicily, for that matter. It just stinks of the classics.

"Anyway, it was fairly late in the afternoon when we came

opposite the city and crept in next to the mole and sneaked through. We were fixed to run if anything shot at us, but nothing did. We went into the harbor and it was really shot to pieces. There were ships sunk all over and twisted cranes and one little Italian destroyer lying over on its side.

"The Air Force really did a job on the waterfront there. Buildings and docks and machinery and boats just blasted into junk. What a junkman's dream that was! What made me think of it was that the water was oily from the blasted ships and there was a dead woman floating on the oily water, face down and with her hair fanned out and floating behind her. She bobbed up and down when our wake spread out in the harbor.

"At first," the captain said, "I didn't know what gave me a queer feeling and then it came to me. There wasn't anybody moving about on the shore at all. You take a wrecked city, why, there's usually someone poking around. But not here. I got the idea I'd like to go ashore. So the First I had then and I, we pulled up between two wrecked fishing boats and we got out a tommy gun apiece and we tied up and jumped ashore.

"It's kind of hard to imagine. Palermo is a pretty big city. Except for the harbor and the waterfront, our bombers hadn't hurt it very much. Oh, there were some wrecks, but not to amount to anything. I tell you, there wasn't one living soul in that city. The population moved right out into the hills and the troops hadn't come yet. There wasn't a soul.

"You'd walk up a street where there were big houses and the doors would be open and—just not anybody. I did see a cat go streaking across the street, a pure white cat, but that's the only living thing there was.

"You know those little painted carts the Sicilians have, with scenes painted on them? Well, there were some of those lying on their sides and the donkeys that pulled them were lying there dead, too.

"The First and I walked up into the town. Every once in a while I'd get the idea of going into one of the houses and just seeing what they were like, but I couldn't. It was quiet and there wasn't a breath of wind and the doors were open and I just couldn't make myself go into one of those houses.

"We'd walked quite a good distance up into the town, farther than we thought, when it began to get dark. Neither of us had thought to bring a flashlight. Well, when we saw the dark coming, I think we both got panicky without any reason. We started to walk back to the waterfront and we kept going faster and faster and then we finally broke into a run.

"There was something about that town that didn't want us there after dark. The open doors were black already and the deep shadows were falling. We dog-trotted through the narrow streets and then I got to thinking—there's nobody here, but now if I see anybody it's going to scare me. It gets dark awfully quick there. It was pitch black in the narrow streets, but you could see light above the houses.

"It got so we were really running and when we broke out on the dock and climbed over the wrecks, we were panting. The First said to me, 'A guy might have got lost in there and not got back all night.' But he knew we had been scared, and I knew it too."

A hard dash of spray came over the bow of the PT and splashed him in the face.

"That gave me the willies," the captain said. "I think that

scared me more than I've been scared for a long time. I got to thinking about it and once or twice I had a dream about it. Come to think of it, the whole thing was like a dream anyway, from that dead woman right on through. But if I ever wanted to say how it was to be alone and panicky, I think I'd think of that right away."

*   *

SOUVENIR

SOMEWHERE IN THE MEDITERRANEAN WAR THEATER, *October 12, 1943*—It is said, and with some truth, that while the Germans fight for world domination and the English for the defense of England, the Americans fight for souvenirs. This may not be the final end for our dogfaces, but it helps. It is estimated that two divisions of American troops could carry away the Great Pyramid, chip by chip, in twenty-four hours. This writer has seen pup tents piled nearly to the ridge rope with nearly valueless mementos of places the soldiers occupied. Dark back rooms of houses in Algiers and Palermo and Messina, and by now probably Salerno, are roaring with the industry of making bits of colored cloth and celluloid into gadgets to sell the soldiers.

A soldier has been seen struggling down a street in Palermo

carrying a fifty-pound statuette of an angel in plaster of Paris. It was painted blue and pink and had written on its base in gold paint, "Balcome too Palermo." How he ever expected to get it home no one will ever know. If the homes of America ever receive the souvenirs that are being collected by our troops there will be no room for living. The post office at an African station recently stopped a sentimental present a soldier was sending his wife. It was a prized possession and he had bought it from a Goum for 1000 francs. It was a quart jar of fingers pickled in brandy.

It is reported that the pre-Roman Greek temples at Salerno have suffered more from chipping by American soldiers in two weeks than they did during the preceding three thousand years, and whereas they have suffered the destructive rage of invaders for centuries they are not expected to survive the admiring souvenir-hunting of our troops, who only want to send a small chip home to the little woman.

True souvenir-hunting has its rules. It does not apply to the fighter group who transported a grand piano, piece by piece, over a thousand miles. Nor to the bomber swing band who rescued a crushed bull fiddle and mended it with airplane fix-it until it was four inches thick. They wanted to use these things. Souvenir hunting, if properly done, only takes notice of things that can't possibly be used for anything at all and are too big or too fragile ever to get home.

Probably the greatest souvenir hunter of this whole war is a private first class who must be nameless but is generally called Bugs.

Bugs, when the battle for Gela in Sicily had abated, was poking about among the ruins, when he came upon a mirror —but such a mirror as to amaze him. It had survived bombing and shellfire in some miraculous manner, a matter which created wonder in Bugs. The mirror was six feet two in height and four feet wide, and it was in a frame of carved and painted wood which represented hundreds of small cupids wrestling and writhing about a length of blue ribbon, which accidentally managed to cover every cupid from indecency. The whole thing must have weighed about seventy-five pounds, and it was so beautiful that it broke Bugs's heart. He just couldn't leave it behind.

Bugs probably fought the toughest war in all Sicily, for he carried the mirror on his back the whole way. When the shellfire was bad, he turned his mirror face down and covered it with dirt. On advances he left it and always came back in the night and got it again, although it entailed marching twice as far as the rest of his outfit.

Finally Bugs arranged a kind of sling, so that while advancing he had the appearance of a charging billboard. He gradually came to devote a good part of his life to the care, transportation, and protection of the biggest souvenir in the whole Seventh Army. When he finally marched into Palermo he did so in triumph, for his mirror was unchipped and its frame was only a little chewed up from handling.

Now, for the first time, Bugs was billeted in a house, one of those tall houses with iron balconies and narrow stairs. Bugs tried in vain to get the mirror around a corner of the narrow stairway and finally he got a rope and, tying one end of it to the balcony, he went back to the street and tied the other end of it to his mirror. Then he went back and hauled it up to the second floor, where he was billeted. There he surveyed the room and decided where to hang his mirror. He drove a nail in the wall, hung the mirror, and stepped back to admire it. And he had just stepped clear when the nail pulled out and the whole thing crashed and broke into a million pieces.

Bugs regarded the mess sadly, but then the great philosophy of the "blowed in the glass" souvenir-hunter took possession of him. He said, "Oh, well, maybe it wouldn't have looked good in our flat, anyways."

*   *

WELCOME

SOMEWHERE IN THE MEDITERRANEAN WAR THEATER, *October 14, 1943*—The Italian people may greet conquering American and British troops with different methods in different parts of the country, but they act always with enthusiasm that amounts to violence. One of their methods makes soldiers a little self-conscious until they get used to it. Great crowds of people stand on the sidewalks as the troops march by and simply applaud by clapping their hands as though they applauded a show. This makes the troops walk very stiffly, smiling self-consciously, half soldiers and half actors.

But this hand-clapping is the most restrained thing that they do. The soldiers get most embarrassed when they are overwhelmed by Italian men who rush up to them, over-power them with embraces, and plant great wet kisses on their cheeks, crying a little as they do it. A soldier hates to push them away, but he is not used to being kissed by men, and all he can do is to blush and try to get away as quick as possible.

A third method of showing enthusiasm at being conquered is to throw any fruit or vegetable which happens to be in season at the occupying troops. In Sicily the grapes were ripe and many a soldier got a swipe across the face with a heavy bunch of grapes tossed with the best will in the world.

The juice ran down inside their shirts, and after a march of a few blocks troops would be pretty well drenched in grape juice, which, incidentally, draws flies badly, and there is nothing to do about it. You can't drown such enthusiasm by making them not throw grapes.

One of the most ridiculous and most dangerous occupations, however, was the investment and capture of the island of Ischia. There the people, casting about for some vegetable or floral tribute, found that the most prominent and showy flower of the season was the pink amaryllis. This is not a pleasant flower at the best, but in the hands of an enthusiastic Italian crowd it can almost be a lethal weapon.

A reasonable-sized bunch of amaryllis, with big, thick stems, may weigh four pounds. In a short drive through the streets of the city of Ischia, some of the troops were nearly beaten to death with flowers, while one naval officer was knocked clear out of a car by a well-aimed bouquet of these terrible flowers. His friends proposed him for a Purple Heart, and wrote a report on his bravery in action. "Under a deadly hail of amaryllis," the report said, "Lieutenant Commander So-and-So fought his way through the street, although badly wounded by this new and secret weapon." A man could easily be killed by an opponent armed with amaryllis.

The pressures on the Italians must have been enormous. They seem to go to pieces emotionally when the war is really and truly over for them. Groups of them simply stand and cry—men, women, and children. They want desperately to do something for the troops and they haven't much to work with. Bottles of wine, flowers, any kind of little gift. They rush to the churches and pray, and then, being afraid to miss something, they rush back to watch more troops. The Italian soldiers in Italy respond instantly to an order to deliver their arms. They pile their rifles up in the streets so quickly that you have the idea they are greatly relieved to get the damned things out of their hands once for all.

But whatever may have been true about the Fascist government, it is instantly obvious that the Italian little people were never our enemies. Whole towns could not put on such acts if they did not mean it. But in nearly every community you will find a fat and sleek man, sometimes a colonel, sometimes a civil administrator. Now and then he wears the silver dagger with the gold tip on the scabbard, which indicates that he was one who marched on Rome with Mussolini.

In a country which has been hungry this man is well fed and beautifully dressed. He has been living on these people since Fascism came here, and he has not done badly for himself. On the surrender of a community he is usually the first to offer to help in the government. He will do anything to help if only he can just keep his graft and his power.

It is to be hoped that he is never permitted either to help or to stay in his position. Indeed, our commanders are usually visited by committees of townspeople and farmers who ask that the local Fascist be removed and kept under wraps.

They know that if he ever gets power again he will avenge himself on them. They hate him and want to be rid of him. And if you ask if they were Fascists, most Italians will reply, "Sure, you were a Fascist or you didn't get any work, and if you didn't work your family starved." And whether or not this is true, they seem to believe it thoroughly.

As the conquest goes on up the length of Italy, the crops are going to change. Some soldiers are already feeling an apprehension for the cabbage districts and the potato harvest, if they too are used as thrown tokens of love and admiration.

*　　　*

THE LADY PACKS

SOMEWHERE IN THE MEDITERRANEAN WAR THEATER, *October 15, 1943*—There is a little island very close to the mainland near Naples which has on it a very large torpedo works, one of the largest in Italy. When Italy had surrendered, the Germans took the island, mined it thoroughly, and ran the detonating wires under the water to the mainland, so that they could blow up the torpedo works if it seemed likely to be captured. The Germans left a few guards, heavily armed, and they also left an Italian admiral and his wife as a sort of hostage to the explosives planted all over the little island.

To a small Anglo-American naval force a curious order came. One single torpedo boat was to take on some British commandos, who were to go ashore in secrecy, cut the wires to the mainland, kill the German guards, and evacuate the Italian admiral and his wife.

The boat assigned was a motor torpedo boat and it lay alongside a pier in the afternoon and waited for the commandos to come aboard. The celebrated commandos, the great swashbucklers, took their time in arriving. In fact, they arrived nearly at dusk, five of them, which to their mind is a large military force. And these were very strange men.

They were small, tired-looking men who might have been waiters or porters at a railroad station. Their backs were slightly bent and their knees knobby and they walked with a shuffling gait. Their huge shoes, with thick rubber soles, looked far too large for them. They were dressed in faded shorts and open shirts, and their arms were an old-fashioned revolver and a long, wicked knife for each. Their leader looked like a weary and petulant mouse who wanted more than anything else in the world to get back to a good safe job in an insurance office with the certainty that his pension would not be held up.

These five monsters came shambling aboard and went immediately below decks to get a cup of tea and a slice of that cake which tastes a little like fish. They sat mournfully in

174

the tiny wardroom, mooning over their tea and scratching the mosquito bites on their lumpy knees.

When it was dark the MTB slipped from the dock and crept out to sea toward the island. The moon was very bright and had to be taken into account. But it was thought that in the indefinite light the action would be easier to accomplish. The motors were muffled, and the small, powerful boat pushed quietly through a smooth, moonlit sea.

On the deck the rubber boat which was to take the raiders ashore was inflated and ready. The gun crew sat quietly at their stations. Just before midnight the boat lay to, and the black outline of the island was not far ahead. Then the commandos came stumbling out of the companionway and stood about on the deck. The captain of the torpedo boat said, "You have all the plans now—cut the wires, kill the guards if possible, and bring out the admiral and his lady. How long do you think that will take you?"

The leader of the commandos gave the subject his consideration, tapping his lips with his finger. "We should be back in an hour," he said at last.

"An hour? Why, it can't take that long. If you take that long you won't be able to do it at all."

"Oh, the guards business and the wires," the commandos explained, "that won't take long."

"What will, then?" the captain demanded.

"Well, the admiral's wife will need time to pack," the commando said. "She doesn't know we're coming. She won't have her things ready." And with that they laid the rubber boat over the side and paddled silently away.

For an hour the MTB lay in the moonlight, waiting. The

sailors kept close watch on the dark island and nothing happened. There were no shots, there were no lights on the blacked-out island. The whole thing was dead and quiet in the misty moonlight.

At ten minutes of the hour the captain began to look at his watch every half-minute, and he muttered to himself about E-boat patrols and the necessity for not putting his ship in danger for nonsense. If there had been any activity ashore he would at least know there was fighting of some kind.

At five minutes of the hour a big shape showed on the water, and because everything is potentially dangerous the gunners swung their machine guns on it and waited for it to identify itself. It approached, and it was a rubber boat. It gently nudged the side of the MTB and a little, slender woman was helped over the side, and then a quite stout admiral in a beautiful overcoat, although the night was warm. These figures went immediately below, but the leader of the commandos said, "Bert, you will go back with me." Three of the men climbed aboard the MTB, and the rubber boat shoved off again and moved back toward the island.

The three remaining commandos stood limply on the deck. The MTB captain was impatient. "Accomplish the mission?" he asked.

"Yes, sir, there were eight guards, not seven."

"You didn't take them?"

"No, sir."

The captain's eyes went quickly to the long, thin knife at the man's belt, and the commando nervously, almost apologetically, fingered its steel hilt.

"What have they gone back for?"

"The lady's trunk, sir. We couldn't get it in the boat. There wasn't room with the rest of us. They've gone back for her trunk. Quite a large one. Old-fashioned kind with a hump on it, you know."

The captain put his hands on his hips and studied the little man.

"Sir?" the commando began.

"Yes, I know. And I wish it was beer, but there isn't any." He called softly into the companionway, "Joel, oh, Joel, get some water on. There'll be five teas wanted in a moment."

*   *

CAPRI

SOMEWHERE IN THE MEDITERRANEAN WAR THEATER, *October 18, 1943*—The day after the island of Capri was taken and before any of the admirals and generals had found it necessary to inspect the defenses of its rocky cliffs and hazardous wine cellars a group of sailors from a destroyer in the harbor strolled along one of the beautiful tree-lined paths. They were inspecting defenses too, the island's and their own, and they found their own lacking in initiative. The hill was steep and there were gardens above and below the path.

As they strolled along a shrill little voice came from under a grape arbor below the way. "I say," said the voice.

The naval men looked over the low wall and saw a tiny old woman—a little bit of a woman—dressed in black, who came scrambling from under the grapevines and climbed up the steps like a puppy. She was breathless.

"I hope you won't mind," she panted. "It was very good to hear English spoken. I am English, you know."

She paused to let this tremendous fact sink in. She was dressed in decent and aging black. She never had made the slightest concession to Italy. Her costume would have done her honor and protected her from scandal in Finchley.

Her eyes danced with pleasure, wise, small, humorous eyes. "They speak Italian here," she said brightly, and it was obvious that she did not if she could help it. "And the Germans came," she said, "and I haven't heard much English. That is why I should like just to hear you talk. I like Americans," she explained, and you could see that she was willing to take any kind of criticism for this attitude. "I haven't heard any English. The Germans came, but I said that, didn't I? Well, anyway, the war came and I couldn't get out, and that is three years, isn't it? And do you know it has been a year since I have had a cup of tea, over a year—you will hardly believe that."

The communications officer said, "We have tea aboard. I could bring you a packet this afternoon."

The little woman danced from one foot to the other like a child. "N-o-o-o," she said excitedly. "Why—what fun, what fun."

Signals said, "Is there anything else you need, because maybe I could bring that to you too?"

For a moment the old bright eyes surveyed him, measuring him. "You couldn't—" she began, and paused. "You couldn't bring a little pat of—butter?"

"Sure I could," said Signals.

"N-o-o-o," she cried, and she began to hop like a child at hopscotch. She held up a finger. "If you'll bring me a little pat of butter I will make some scones, real scones, and we'll have a party. Won't that be fun? Won't that be fun?"

She danced with excitement. "Imagine," she said.

"I'll bring it this afternoon," said Signals.

"You see, I was caught here and then the Germans came. They didn't do me really any harm. They were just here," she said seriously. "All of my people are in Australia. I have no family in England any more." Her old eyes became sad without any transition. "I don't know how they are," she said. "I have had two letters in three years. It takes nearly a year to get a letter."

Signals said, "If you will write a letter I'll pick it up when I bring the butter and tea and will mail it at the first port."

She looked at him sternly. "And how long will that take to get to Australia?" she demanded.

"Oh, I don't know. A few weeks."

"No-o-o-o," she cried, and she began to dance again, little dainty dancing steps, with her arms held slightly out from her sides and her wrists bent down. Her shrill little bird voice laughed and her pale old eyes were wet. "Why," she cried. "Why, that will be more fun than tea."

*   *

SEA WARFARE

SOMEWHERE IN THE MEDITERRANEAN WAR THEATER, *October 19, 1943*—The plans for Task Force X were nearly complete. The officers had coffee in a restaurant in a North African city. The tall, nervous one, a lieutenant commander and a student of mines—contact, magnetic, and those vibration mines which react to the engine of a ship—leaned over the table.

"I conceive naval warfare to be much like chamber music," he said. "Thirty-caliber machine guns, those are the violins, the fifties are the violas, six-inch guns are perfect cellos."

He looked a little sad. "I've never had sixteen-inch guns to compose with. I have never had any bass." He leaned back in his chair. "The composition—the tactics of chamber music —are much the same as a well-conceived and planned naval engagement. Destroyers out, why, that will be the statement of theme, the screening attack, and all preparing for the great statement of the battleships." He leaned back farther and tipped his chair against the wall and hooked his heels over the lower rung.

A lieutenant (j.g.) laughed. "He always talks like that. If he didn't know so much about mines we would think he was crazy."

"You haven't been in battle, in a good naval engagement, and you don't know anything about chamber music," said the lieutenant commander. "I'll show you something tonight if you'll go with me."

The jeep moved through the blackout. The streets of the city were lined with military trucks and heavy equipment, all moving toward the harbor where the ships were loading for Italy. The jeep, running counter to the traffic, climbed the hill and went over the ridge and into the valley on the other side, into a valley which had at one time been a place of vineyards and small country houses. But now it was a vast storage ground for shells and trucks and tanks, lined and stacked and parked, waiting to get aboard the ships for Italy. The moon lighted the masses of material getting ready for war.

"Where are you taking us?" the lieutenant asked.

"You'll see. Just be patient."

The jeep pulled up to a very white wall that extended off into the distance and disappeared into the pearly indefiniteness of the moonlight. A high gate of iron bars and spikes opened in the wall. The lieutenant commander went to the gate and pulled a rope that hung there, and a small bell called softly. In a moment a white-robed figure appeared at the gate, a tall man with a long, dark beard.

"Yes?" he asked softly.

"May we come in?" the lieutenant commander asked. "May we come in for evensong?"

"Yes, of course," the brother said. He pulled at one side of the gate and the hinges cried a little.

Inside the wall was a lovely garden in the moonlight. No war material at all. Everything was cut out except flowers and the little sound of running water and the thick outline of a sturdy church against a luminous sky. The lieutenant (j.g.) said, "You speak very good English."

"I should," said the brother. "I was born in Massachusetts."

"American?"

"We come from all over. We have Germans and French, and even a Chinese. Some Russians, too."

The party moved slowly up the path and came to the little fountain which made the dripping sound and put a cool emphasis on a hot night. "The song has already started," the brother said. "Walk quietly."

The way went among the walls of flowering shrubs and then up two outside steps, and then into a dark hallway, and finally through an entrance into a place that was familiar and strange. Over the rail and below was the body of the church, only you could not see it, for only one candle was burning, and it merely suggested the size and height. It picked out a corner and an arch and a point of gold, and your mind filled in the rest. Lined below, just visible, were the rows of the white brothers. And then their voices came softly and swelling, singing the ancient music, the disembodied and unimpassioned music, of which Mozart said he would rather have written one chant than all his own. The evensong rose higher and higher, and it was rather like the dimness of the arched roof overhead. The great, vague room swelled and pulsed with the sound, and then it died and one single voice took it up and the others joined in and the candle flame darted about on its wick.

The sound of the trucks and the half-tracks and the pound of the tanks came vaguely from the distance and the music rose to a high note and stopped. The lines of white figures filed slowly out and a hand came into the candlelight and pinched out the flame.

The jeep went back into the city, and this time it went very slowly because it was caught between a weapons carrier and a troop truck loaded with sleepy, upright soldiers who swayed when the truck struck a rough stretch of street.

The lieutenant (j.g.) was very quiet. Some paradox worried him. He said, "The change from one thing to another was too quick. There was no time to get used to it. You should have time to get used to things like that."

"There was actually no change," the lieutenant commander said. "I've always thought that naval warfare was composed like chamber music. There wasn't any change. You just saw two sides of the same thing. You can't make islands of experiences. They relate just exactly as the strings relate in a quartet. Maybe you'll see in a day or two when we get into action. You haven't been in action, have you?"

*　　　　*

THE WORRIED BARTENDER

SOMEWHERE IN THE MEDITERRANEAN WAR THEATER, *October 20, 1943*—When our small American force had captured the island of Capri with no resistance whatsoever on its part or on ours, it was only natural that sooner or later we should meet Luigi the bartender. Luigi had kept warm during the whole war a love of Americans based, he freely admitted, on a memory of tips in the nicer days when American tourists came to bathe in the Blue Grotto and the pink wine. When sailors and officers from the little force inspected the defenses of Luigi's bar and found them formidable, Luigi was cordial but sad. He spoke the English we know, the English of the banana pushcarts and the pizzerias, of the spaghetti joints and grind organs. Luigi's dialect sounded like home.

Luigi was gay but sad. His joy had a habit of falling off in the middle and dissipating. One afternoon, after each one of us had tried to remember a man named Giuseppe Marinari, of Gary, Indiana, who was Luigi's third cousin, we inquired into his sadness. And only then did his trouble come out with a rush.

It seemed that Luigi had a daughter and, more than that, he had an incipient grandchild. But this daughter and this expectation were across the little stretch of water in Castellammare. And what was worse, the Germans were moving up on Castellammare and we were not there in enough force either to repel or to intercept them. Consequently it seemed that Luigi's daughter was very likely to have her child in a shell hole, illuminated by star shells and parachute flares and possibly speeded up by bomb bursts. Luigi was worried and upset because, he explained, it was not as though he had other daughters or grandchildren. This was his sole chick, due to some misfortune or deformity, the reason for which was known only to God. And as Luigi poured out his story he also poured out Scotch whisky that had been buried in the earth in back of his bar ever since the war started.

Going back to the ship, the little group could not lose the sadness that Luigi had planted in it. "How would you like it to happen to your family?" Lieutenant Blank said. "Why, you can look across to Castellammare."

On this basis the group visited the commodore in the wardroom of his flagship. They told their story and the commodore looked gravely over his coffee cup at them. And his very calm blue eyes got bright with amusement. "What do you want me to do," he asked, "attack Castellammare?"

"No, sir," said Lieutenant Blank. "But we have six captured Italian MS boats. How would it be if we took one of them and just went over and got her? It would only take an hour or less."

"And suppose you lost the boat and got yourself killed?"

"We wouldn't do that, sir. We would just run over and get her. We could do it in practically a few minutes."

The commodore said, "I can't permit it. The thing is out of the question. The thing is silly. We're trying to run a war, not a maternity hospital. And besides, I have work for you to do. You can't go running about like this."

"Yes, sir," said Lieutenant Blank.

"These are your orders," said the commodore. "You are to take one of the MS boats and patrol the coast of the mainland, particularly in the area about Castellammare. You will report the presence of any German shipping there and if you see any hostile craft you will report it and engage it. It may be necessary for you to go pretty far inshore to carry out these orders. Do you understand?"

"Yes, sir," said Lieutenant Blank, "but I sure wish we could have got that girl off."

"This is no time for sentiment," the commodore said.

The thing was very quick. It required only to pull up to the little dock at the little town and to ask for Luigi's daughter. In ten minutes she was at the dock carrying a bundle of clothing and, in our estimation, she was a little closer than even Luigi suspected. And then the Isotta-Fraschini engines of the MS boat purred and the white wake spread away from the boat and she cut through the water back to Capri, for MS boats do not ride on top of the water, they knife through it.

The rest was very silly. Luigi was at the waterfront and he cried and his daughter cried and about a thousand Caprianos cried and the sound of kissing was deafening and a lot of sailors looked gruff and a kind of triumphant procession went up the hill on the funicular railway and there was something in the nature of a party at Luigi's bar. The child, no matter what its sex, is going to have Lieutenant Blank's first name, and not only Luigi but all Luigi's relatives are going to remember all of us in their prayers for hundreds of years to come.

So much for the assurances. But the next morning a party of five went up on the hill to get haircuts. We were sitting reading copies of *The London Pictorial* for 1937 and waiting for the one barber chair to be vacant when in the doorway Luigi appeared. And Luigi carried a little tray and on the tray was a Scotch and soda for each of us. And later in the day we went shopping and wherever we stopped to look and to buy there Luigi appeared with his little tray.

It was a pretty nice day.

*   *

THE CAMERA MAKES SOLDIERS

SOMEWHERE IN THE MEDITERRANEAN WAR THEATER, *October 21, 1943*—I suppose that there is no weapon which so slyly and surely attacks the souls of men as a moving-picture camera does. Men who are disgusted or hurt or just plain ignorant react to a Bell & Howell Eyemo as a frog does to a hot rock. One of out best sports writers suggested one time that the best way to get touchdowns in football was to mount a newsreel camera between the goal posts. It is a secret weapon which dissects people and brings out the curious childish ego that everyone has and lays it spread out thick on the surface.

Recently in Africa and Sicily and Italy we (not editorial we, but a cameraman and I) were working on a technical picture for the Army and there we discovered that the same force that operates at Long Island garden parties and at tennis matches also works on a battle line. It worked everywhere. Weary troops straightened up and marched stiffly and some of them tried to hog the camera and some of them looked fierce and soldierly. All shoulders went back and steps quickened. The thinly covered actor in everyone came out. A line of Army stevedores on a dock in a North African port suddenly, on seeing the camera, began to pass boxes of C-rations with a speed and rhythm which has probably never been duplicated in Army history. Of course the moment the camera was moved they went back to a much more sensible, goldbricking pace, but for the few feet of film we have, the boxes shot by and piled up in a mountain out of camera range.

The impact of the camera is by no means limited to the Americans. Our picture had to do with all kinds of work and all kinds of men. One day we set up on a barge where a number of Arabs were employed to unload cargo and, incidentally, were doing the finest bit of sleepwalking I have ever seen. Each Arab regarded each box as a personality he didn't like, touched with reluctance, and got rid of with relief. His repugnance, however, did not make him carry it to its destination with any speed that required streamlining. With these people we did not find any speed-up when the camera was produced. The moment it began to turn, every Arab stood up grandly and presented his profile and looked sternly toward Mecca. Time and time again we tried to catch them in what is called a natural pose, not of work, because that would be a contradiction in terms, but just relaxed and looking Arab. But either they had seen too many Hollywood films of Valentino as an Arab, or Valentino had studied Arabs under the impact of the camera. We never caught them any other way except looking sternly offstage, always in profile and always noble. We had wanted to get them relaxed because I suppose Arabs have as few noble moments as anyone in the world. Bushmen may compete with them in this respect but I doubt it. And they could not be fooled. They knew when the camera was turning and when it wasn't. They were as highly trained in stealing scenes from each other as dress extras in Hollywood. Finally we gave up. They will continue noble as far as we are concerned. We will perpetuate this myth of the noble Arab. The moment we stopped shooting they collapsed into natural Arabs, but we never got it on film.

The camera works everywhere. There is no ferocity like that on the face of a quarterback who is running, not at an opponent but at newsreel coverage on a tripod. And this may all be egotism, but there was one example of something that seemed to be much more than this. One day we set up the camera to photograph the discharge of the cargo of a hospital ship which had been loaded in Sicily. The side doors of the ship were opened and the wooden platform was extended. The lines of ambulances were drawn up on the pier, and then the stretcher-bearers came down in a steady line with the wounded men sitting and lying and huddled and stretched out in positions indicated by the nature of their wounds. Some of them were sick with pain, were gray with pain, and some were only slightly hurt so that their eyes were clear. And not one single man as he passed the camera failed to respond to it. Everyone gave it either a smile or a little nod. Some saluted it gravely. The rigid features changed and the eyes brightened, and if an arm could move it moved in greeting. I think this was not egotism. I think these men, each one of them, had a quick thought. "Someone at home will see this picture. I must appear less badly hurt than I am. Otherwise they might worry." I think those tired smiles were a great hunk of consideration and courage.

*   *

THE STORY OF AN ELF

Monday, November 1, 1943—This story could not be written if there were not witnesses—not vague unknown men, but Quentin Reynolds and H. R. Knickerbocker and Clark Lee and Jack Belden, who was hurt at Salerno, and John Lardner and a number of others who will come clamoring forward if anyone doubts the facts here to be presented.

The thing began when a British consul met Quentin Reynolds in the hall of the Alletti Hotel in Algiers. The consul was a small, innocent, well-mannered man who liked to think of the British and Americans as allies and who was willing to make amicable gestures. In good faith he asked Reynolds where he was staying and in equal good faith Reynolds replied that he had not yet been billeted.

"There's an extra bed in my room," the consul said. "You're welcome to it if you like."

That was the beginning, and what happened was nobody's fault. It was just one of those accidents. The consul had a nice room with a balcony that overlooked the harbor and from which you could watch air raids. It wasn't Reynolds' fault. He accepted hospitality for himself, not for the nine other war correspondents who moved in with him. Nine is only a working number. Sometimes there were as many as eighteen. They slept on the floor, on the balcony, in the bathroom, and some even slept in the hall outside the door of Room 140, Alletti Hotel, Algiers.

It was generally agreed that the consul should have his own bed, that is, if he kept it. But let him get up to go to the bathroom and he returned to find Knickerbocker or Lee or Belden, or all three, in it. Another thing bothered the consul a little. Correspondents don't sleep much at night. They talked and argued and sang so that the poor consul didn't get much rest. There was too much going on in his room. He had to work in the daytime, and he got very little sleep at night. Toward the end of the week he took to creeping back in the middle of the afternoon for a nap. He couldn't get his bed then. Someone always had it. But at three in the afternoon it was usually quiet enough so that he could curl up on the floor and get a little rest.

The foregoing is not the unbelievable part—quite the contrary. It is what follows that will require witnesses. It was during one of the all-night discussions of things in general that someone, perhaps Clark Lee, perhaps Dour Jack Belden, suggested that we were getting very tired of Algerian wine and wouldn't it be nice if we had some Scotch. From that point on this is our story and we intend to stick to it.

Someone must have rubbed something, a ring or a lamp or perhaps the utterly exhausted British consul. At any rate, there was a puff of blue smoke and standing in the room was a small man with pointed ears and a very jolly stomach. He wore a suit of green leather and his cap and the toes of his shoes ended in sharp points and they were green too.

"Saints of Galway," said Reynolds. "Do you see what I see?"

"Yes," said Clark Lee.

"Well, do you believe it?"

"No," said Lee, who is after all a realist and was at Corregidor.

Jack Belden has lived in China for many years and he knows about such things. "Who are you?" he asked sternly.

"I'm little Charley Lytle," the elf said.

"Well, what do you want, popping in on us?" Belden cried.

The British consul groaned and turned over and pulled the covers over his head. Knickerbocker has since admitted that his first impulse was to kill the elf and stuff him to go beside the sailfish in his den. In fact, he was creeping up when Charley Lytle held up his hand.

"When war broke out I tried to enlist," he said. "But I was

rejected on political grounds. It isn't that I have any politics," he explained. "But the Army's position is that if I did have, heaven knows what they would be. There hasn't been a Republican leprechaun since Coolidge. So I was rejected pending the formation of an Elves-in-Exile Battalion. I decided then that I would just make people happy, soldiers and war correspondents and things like that."

Reynolds' eyes narrowed dangerously. He is very loyal. "Are you insinuating that we aren't happy?" he gritted. "That my friends aren't happy?"

"I'm not happy," said the British consul, but no one paid any attention to him.

Little Charley Lytle said, "I heard some mention made of Scotch whisky. Now it just happens that I have—"

"How much?" said Clark Lee, who is a realist.

"Why, all you want."

"I mean how much money?" Lee demanded.

"You don't understand," said little Charley. "There is no money involved. It is my contribution to the war—I believe you call it *effort*."

"I'm going to kill him," cried Knickerbocker. "Nobody can sneer at my war and get away with it."

Reynolds said, "Could we get a case?"

"Surely," said little Charley.

"Three cases?"

"Certainly."

Lee broke in. "Now don't you strain him. You don't know what his breaking point is."

"When can you deliver?" Reynolds asked.

Instead of answering, little Charley Lytle made a dramatic and slightly ribald gesture. There was one puff of smoke and he had disappeared. There followed three small explosions, like a series of tiny depth charges, and on the floor of Room 140 of the Alletti Hotel in Algiers lay three cases of Haig and Haig Pinch Bottle, ringed with the hot and incredulous eyes of a platoon of thirsty correspondents.

Reynolds breathed heavily the way a man does when he has a stroke. "A miracle!" he whispered. "A miracle straight out of the middle ages or Mary Roberts Rinehart."

Dour Jack Belden has lived a long time in China. On top of a basic pessimism, he has seen everything and is difficult to impress. His eyes now wandered out the arched window to the sweltering streets and the steaming harbor below. "It's a medium good trick," he said. "But it's a cold-weather trick. I'd like to give him a real test." He ignored the growl of growing rage from his peers. "If this so-called Elf could produce a bottle of say La Batt's Pale India Ale on a day like this, I'd say he was a commer—" He was interrupted by a slight fall of snow from the hot and fly-specked ceiling. Our eyes followed the lazy white flakes to the floor, where they fell on a box of slim-necked bottles. The snow swirled and spelled out *Courtesy of Canada* in the air.

I think Jack Belden went too far. He said lazily, "But is it cold?"

Reynolds flung himself forward and touched the neck of a bottle. "Colder than a (two words deleted by censor)," he said.

That night there was an air raid, and even the British consul enjoyed it. And anyone who doesn't believe this story can ask any of the people involved, even dour Jack Belden.

*   *

MAGIC PIECES

November 3, 1943—A great many soldiers carry with them some small article, some touchstone or lucky piece or symbol which, if they are lucky in battle, takes on an ever-increasing importance. And being lucky in battle means simply not being hurt. The most obvious magic amulets, of course, are the rabbits' feet on sale in nearly all gift stores. St. Christopher medals are carried by Catholics and non-Catholics alike and in many cases are not considered as religious symbols at all, but as simple lucky pieces.

A novelty company in America has brought out a Testament bound in steel covers to be carried in the shirt pocket over the heart, a gruesome little piece of expediency which has faith in neither the metal nor the Testament but hopes that a combination may work. Many of these have been sold to parents of soldiers, but I have never seen one carried. That particular pocket is for cigarettes and those soldiers who carry Testaments, as many do, carry them in their pants pockets, and they are never considered as lucky pieces.

The magic articles are of all kinds. There will be a smooth stone, an odd-shaped piece of metal, small photographs encased in cellophane. Many soldiers consider pictures of their wives or parents to be almost protectors from danger. One soldier had removed the handles from his Colt .45 and had carved new ones out of Plexiglass from a wrecked airplane. Then he had installed photographs of his children under the Plexiglass so that his children looked out of the handles of his pistol.

Sometimes coins are considered lucky and rings and pins, usually articles which take their quality from some intimacy with people at home, a gift or the symbol of some old emotional experience. One man carries a locket his dead wife wore as a child and another a string of amber beads his mother once made him wear to ward off colds. The beads now ward off danger.

It is interesting that, as time in action goes on, these magics not only become more valuable and dear but become more secret also. And many men make up small rituals to cause their amulets to become active. A smooth stone may be rubbed when the tracers are cutting lines about a man's head. One sergeant holds an Indian-head penny in the palm of his left hand and against the stock of his rifle when he fires. He is just about convinced that he cannot miss if he does this. The employment of this kind of magic is much more widespread than is generally known.

As time goes on, and dangers multiply and perhaps there is a narrow escape or so, the amulet not only takes on an increasing importance but actually achieves a kind of personality. It becomes a thing to talk to and rely on. One such lucky piece is a small wooden pig only about an inch long. Its owner, after having tested it over a period of time and in one or two tight places, believes that this little wooden pig can accomplish remarkable things. Thus, in a bombing, he held the pig in his hand and said, "Pig, this one is not for us." And in a shelling, he said, "Pig, you know that the one that gets me, gets you."

But in addition to simply keeping its owner safe from harm, this pig has been known to raise a fog, smooth out a high sea, procure a beefsteak in a restaurant which had not had one for weeks. It is rumored further that this pig in the hands of a previous owner has commuted an execution, cured assorted cases of illness, and been the direct cause of at least one considerable fortune. This pig's owner would not part with him for anything.

The association between a man and his amulet becomes not only very strong but very private. This is partly a fear of being laughed at, but also a feeling grows that to tell about it is to rob it of some of its powers. Also there is the feeling that the magic must not be called on too often. The virtue of the piece is not inexhaustible. It can run down, therefore it is better to use it sparingly and only to call on it when the need is great.

Novelty companies have taken advantage of this almost universal urge toward magic. They turn out lucky rings by the thousands and coins and little figures, but these have never taken hold the way the associational gadgets do.

Whatever the cause of this reliance on magic amulets, in wartime it is so. And the practice is by no means limited to ignorant or superstitious men. It would seem that in times of great danger and great emotional tumult a man has to reach outside himself for help and comfort, and has to have some supra-personal symbol to hold to. It can be anything at all, an old umbrella handle or a religious symbol, but he has to have it. There are times in war when the sharpest emotion is not fear, but loneliness and littleness. And it is during these times that the smooth stone or the Indian-head penny or the wooden pig are not only desirable but essential. Whatever atavism may call them up, they appear and they seem to fill a need. The dark world is not far from us—from any of us.

*   *

SYMPTOMS

November 5, 1943—During the years between the last war and this one, I was always puzzled by the reticence of ex-soldiers about their experiences in battle. If they had been reticent men it would have been different, but some of them were talkers and some were even boasters. They would discuss their experiences right up to the time of battle and then suddenly they wouldn't talk any more. This was considered heroic in them. It was thought that what they had seen or done was so horrible that they didn't want to bring it back to haunt them or their listeners. But many of these men had no such consideration in any other field.

Only recently have I found what seems to be a reasonable explanation, and the answer is simple. They did not and do not remember—and the worse the battle was, the less they remember.

In all kinds of combat the whole body is battered by emotion. The ductless glands pour their fluids into the system to make it able to stand up to the great demand on it. Fear and ferocity are products of the same fluid. Fatigue toxins poison the system. Hunger followed by wolfed food distorts the metabolic pattern already distorted by the adrenalin and fatigue. The body and the mind so disturbed are really ill and fevered. But in addition to these ills, which come from the inside of a man and are given him so that he can temporarily withstand pressures beyond his ordinary ability, there is the further stress of explosion.

Under extended bombardment or bombing the nerve ends are literally beaten. The ear drums are tortured by blast and the eyes ache from the constant hammering.

This is how you feel after a few days of constant firing. Your skin feels thick and insensitive. There is a salty taste in your mouth. A hard, painful knot is in your stomach where the food is undigested. Your eyes do not pick up much detail and the sharp outlines of objects are slightly blurred. Everything looks a little unreal. When you walk, your feet hardly seem to touch the ground and there is a floaty feeling all over your body. Even the time sense seems to be changed. Men who are really moving at a normal pace seem to take forever to pass a given point. And when you move it seems to you that you are very much slowed down, although actually you are probably moving more quickly than you normally do.

Under the blast your eyeballs are so beaten that the earth

and the air seem to shudder. At first your ears hurt, but then they become dull and all your other senses become dull, too. There are exceptions, of course. Some men cannot protect themselves this way and they break, and they are probably the ones we call shell-shock cases.

In the dullness all kinds of emphases change. Even the instinct for self-preservation is dulled so that a man may do things which are called heroic when actually his whole fabric of reaction is changed. The whole world becomes unreal. You laugh at things which are not ordinarily funny and you become enraged at trifles. During this time a kind man is capable of great cruelties and a timid man of great bravery, and nearly all men have resistance to stresses beyond their ordinary ability.

Then sleep can come without warning and like a drug. Gradually your whole body seems to be packed in cotton. All the main nerve trunks are deadened, and out of the battered cortex curious dreamlike thoughts emerge. It is at this time that many men see visions. The eyes fasten on a cloud and the tired brain makes a face of it, or an angel or a demon. And out of the hammered brain strange memories are jolted loose, scenes and words and people forgotten, but stored in the back of the brain. These may not be important things, but they come back with startling clarity into the awareness that is turning away from reality. And these memories are almost visions.

And then it is over. You can't hear, but there is a rushing sound in your ears. And you want sleep more than anything, but when you do sleep you are dream-ridden, your mind is uneasy and crowded with figures. The anesthesia your body has given you to protect you is beginning to wear off, and, as with most anesthesia, it is a little painful.

And when you wake up and think back to the things that happened they are already becoming dreamlike. Then it is not unusual that you are frightened and ill. You try to remember what it was like, and you can't quite manage it. The outlines in your memory are vague. The next day the memory slips farther, until very little is left at all. A woman is said to feel the same way when she tries to remember what childbirth was like. And fever leaves this same kind of vagueness on the mind. Perhaps all experience which is beyond bearing is that way. The system provides the shield and then removes the memory, so that a woman can have another child and a man can go into combat again.

It slips away so fast. Unless you made notes on the spot you could not remember how you felt or the way things looked. Men in prolonged battle are not normal men. And when afterward they seem to be reticent—perhaps they don't remember very well.

*   *

THE PLYWOOD NAVY

November 15, 1943—The orders were simple. The naval task force was to destroy or drive German shipping out of the sea in the whole area north of Rome. German convoys were moving out of various ports, possibly evacuating heavy equipment from Italy to the south of France. The task force was ordered to break up this traffic.

It is not permitted to say what units comprised the force but a part of it at least was a group of torpedo boats, some British MTBs and some American PTs. The British were not quite so fast as the Americans but they were more heavily armed.

The afternoon before the attack was spent in putting the boats ready. The gunners had their guns apart, oiling and scrubbing the salt spray from the working parts. The guns on the little boats must be worked on all the time. Even the cartridge cases turn green from the constant splashing with salt water. The American PTs are wet devils. Any speed of any kind of sea brings green water over the bow. The men dress in rubber clothes and rubber hoods and even then they do not stay dry.

In the afternoon the torpedoes were inspected and the fuel tanks filled to the limit. The sea was very blue and very calm. During the whole first two weeks of the attack against Italy the sea was calm as a lake, and that particular sea can be very bad.

The British officers and men were bearded with fine great brushes which projected forward from constant brushing outward with the hands. This gives a pugnacious look to a man's face. A few American faces were bearded too, but the tradition is not set with our men.

From the little island harbor, the coast of Italy was visible in the afternoon—the steep hills terraced for vines and lemon trees and the mountains rising to bare rocky ridges behind.

Vesuvius was smoking in the background, a high feather of smoke.

On the quay, surrendered Italian carabinieri stood looking at the "Plywood Navy," which is what the crews call the torpedo boats.

As the sun went down the work was finished and dinner was started in the tiny galleys of the Plywood Navy. The force was to sail at dark. Long before dark the moon was up. It would set after two in the morning and it was planned to be on the ground and ready for attack as soon as the moon had set. This was a deadly swarm that prepared to go. In its combined torpedo tubes it carried the force to sink a navy. The little ships can dodge in close and, when the going is rough, they can scatter and run like quail. And they can turn and twist so fast and travel at such speed that they are impossible to catch and very hard to hit.

Just at dusk the motors burst into roars one at a time and then settled down to their throbbing beat. These motors can be quieted so that they make very little noise, but in ordinary running they sound like airplanes.

The moonlit night came, and the little boats moved out from their berths, and once clear of the breakwater they formed in three lines and settled down to traveling speed. In the moonlight their white wakes shone, and each boat ran over the wake of the boat ahead, and the beat of their motors was deep. On the decks the men had already put on their rubber pants and their rubber coats and the peaked rubber hoods. In the turrets the men sat at their machine guns and waited.

On 412 the master and his First stood on the little bridge.

The spray came over the bow in long, swishing spurts as the PT put her nose down into the easy swells and the light wind picked up the splash. Their faces were dripping. Now and then the First stepped the three steps down to the tiny chart room where a hooded light glimmered on the chart. (One line deleted by censor.) The First checked the course and put his head through and climbed back to the bridge. A call came from aft—"Aircraft at nine o'clock!"

The men at the turrets and at the after gun swung their weapons sharp to the left and elevated the muzzles, and the gunners peered uneasily into the milky moonlit sky. Unless they come out of the moon, and they never do, they are very hard to see. But above the engines of the boat could be heard the hum of aircraft engines. "Ours or theirs?" the First asked.

"Ours have orders not to come close. It must be theirs," the master said. Then off to the port side in the milky sky there was the dark shape of a plane and not flying very high. The gunners stirred and followed the shape with the muzzles. It was too far off to fire. The master picked up his megaphone and called, "He'll come in from the side if he's coming. Watch for him." The drone of the plane disappeared.

"Maybe he didn't see us," the First said.

"With our wake? Sure he saw us. Maybe he was one of ours."

He must have cut his motors. Suddenly he is overhead and his bomb lands and explodes just after he has passed over. The roar of the explosion and the battering of the machine guns come at once. A wall of spray comes over the side from the explosion, and the boat seems to leap out of the sea.

The lines of the tracers reach for the disappearing plane and the lines seem to curve the way the stream from a hose does when you move the hose. Then the guns are silent. The master calls, "Watch out for him. He may be back. Watch for him from the same side." The gunners obediently swing their guns about.

This time he didn't cut his motors. Maybe he needed altitude. You could hear him coming. The guns started on him before he was overhead and the curving lines of tracers followed him over and each line was a little bit behind him. And then one line jumped ahead. A little blue light showed on him then. For a moment he seemed to hover and then he fell, end over end, but slowly, and the blue light on him got larger and larger as he came down. The rest of the guns were after him as he came down. He landed about five hundred yards away and the moment he struck the water he broke into a great yellow flame, and then a second later he exploded with a dull boom and the fire was sucked down under the sea and he was gone.

"He must have been crazy," the captain said, "to come in like that. Who got him?" No one answered. The captain called to the port turret, "Did you get him, Ernest?"

"Yes, sir," said Ernest. "I think so."

"Good shooting," said the captain.

*   *

November 19, 1943—Torpedo boat 412 slipped southward. The moon seemed to hang in the sky and to have given up the idea of ever setting. Actually it was time in the mind that was slowed down. The mufflers were still on the engines but the boat picked up a little speed, not the great roaring rush of the wide-open PT but a steady drumming that threw out a curving V of wake and boiled the water a little under the fantail. The captain said, "Keep your eyes peeled for the others. We don't want our own people to smack us." He went down into the little chart room again and studied his charts. Then he poked his head up and spoke to his First. "A port isn't far off now," he said. "Let's get there. We might catch a convoy." On top of his words there came a distant drumming of engines.

The First cut his motors still further to listen, and the speed of the 412 dropped. "I guess those are ours," he said.

The captain cocked his head a little. "Something wrong," he said. "Doesn't sound right." And he cocked his head on the other side, like a listening spaniel. "Ever heard an E-boat?" he asked.

"No, I haven't. You know damn well I haven't."

"Neither have I," said the captain, "but those don't sound like PTs or MTBs to me." He peered over the rail. The signalman had his blinker ready to make a recognition signal. The captain said quickly, "Kill the motor." Through the milky light the E-boats came. They seemed to grow up out of the night, the misty shapes of them high-prowed and unmistakable. The 412 drifted easily in the water.

The captain said hoarsely to the signalman, "Don't signal, for God's sake!" He was silent for a moment and there seemed to be E-boats all around. "Listen," the captain said. "We've maybe got to make a crash run. I don't know when." (Ten lines deleted by censor.)

The E-boats moved slowly past. They must have seen the 412 lying uneasily in the moonlight. Perhaps it didn't occur to them that a hostile craft would lie so still so near to their guns. The breathing of the crew was almost audible. The E-boats were nearly past when one of them, just on the chance, blinked. (One line deleted by censor.) The gunners brought down their barrels. The engines of the 412 roared and the boat leaped in the water. She stood up on her own crest and tore away. (One line deleted by censor.) Her wake in the last of the moonlight was creamy behind her. She whipped over the water like a gull. But the E-boats did not fire on her. They continued placidly on their way.

Five minutes of the run, and the First throttled down and the 412 settled back into the water and leveled out and the sound of her motors died away. "God Almighty," the captain said. And he whistled to himself. "That was close."

(Three lines deleted by censor.) "Let's lie here and get our breath. That was too close."

The moon lay close to the water at last. In a few minutes it would be dark, deliciously dark, safe and dark. The men stirred about nervously on the silent boat.

And then across the moon a dark shape moved and then another. "Good God," the captain said, "there's a convoy. That's what the E-boats were for." A large dark hull moved across the moon. "We've got to get to them," the captain said excitedly.

"They'll get us sure," said the first.

"No they won't." (Three lines deleted by censor.)

He called his orders softly. The torpedo men moved to their places. The 412 turned silently and slipped toward the passing convoy. There seemed to be ships of all sizes, and the 412 could see them against the sinking moon and they could not see the 412. "That big one," the captain said. "She must be at least five thousand tons." He issued his orders and took the wheel himself. Then he swung the boat and called softly, "Fire!" There was a sharp explosive whisk of sound and a splash, and the torpedo was away. He swung again and fired another. And his mouth moved as though he were counting.

Then without warning the sea and the sky tore to pieces in a vomit of light and a moment later the 412 nearly jumped out of the water. "Run," the captain shouted. "Run!" And the 412 leaped up on its fantail again and pushed its bow into the air.

The explosion was gone almost the moment it had started. There wasn't much of any fire. It just subsided and the water closed over it.

"Ammunition," the captain shouted. "Ammunition or high-test gasoline."

But the rest of the fleet was not silent. The tracers reached out for the sea, and the rockets, even the flak rockets. The crossfire reached to sea and combed the sea and searched the sea. (One line deleted by censor.) Some time later the captain touched his First's arm and the First pulled down the boat again. In the distance, as the moon went down, the E-boats were probably beating the ocean looking for the 412 or the submarine or whatever had hit their ship. But the 412 had got away. (One line deleted by censor.) The pitch blackness lay on the water after the moon had gone. Ocean and land and boat were blotted out.

"Let's get the hell out of here," said the captain. "Let's get on back."

*   *

A DESTROYER

November 24, 1943—A destroyer is a lovely ship, probably the nicest fighting ship of all. Battleships are a little like steel cities or great factories of destruction. Aircraft carriers are floating flying fields. Even cruisers are big pieces of machinery, but a destroyer is all boat. In the beautiful clean lines of her, in her speed and roughness, in her curious gallantry, she is completely a ship, in the old sense.

For one thing, a destroyer is small enough so that her captain knows his whole crew personally, knows all about each one as a person, his first name and his children and the trouble he has been in and is capable of getting into. There is an ease on a destroyer that is good and a good relationship among the men. Then if she has a good captain you have something really worth serving on.

The battleships are held back for a killing blow, and such a blow sometimes happens only once in a war. The cruisers go in second, but the destroyers work all the time. They are probably the busiest ships of a fleet. In a major engagement, they do the scouting and make the first contact. They convoy, they run to every fight. Wherever there is a mess, the destroyers run first. They are not lordly like the battleships, nor episcopal like the cruisers. Most of all they are ships and the men who work them are seamen. In rough weather they are rough, honestly and violently rough.

A destroyerman is never bored in wartime, for a destroyer is a seaman's ship. She can get under way at the drop of a hat. The water under fantail boils like a Niagara. She will go rippling along at thirty-five knots with the spray sheeting over her and she will turn and fight and run, drop depth charges, bombard, and ram. She is expendable and dangerous. And because she is all these things, a destroyer's crew is passionately possessive. Every man knows his ship, every inch of it, not just his own station.

The destroyer X is just such a ship. She has done many thousands of miles since the war started. She has been bombed and torpedoes have gone under her bow. She has convoyed and fought. Her captain is a young, dark-haired man and his executive officer looks like a blond undergraduate. The ship is immaculate. The engines are polished and painted and shined.

She is a fairly new ship, the X, commissioned fifteen months ago. She bombarded at Casablanca and Gela and Salerno and she has captured islands. Her officers naturally would like to go to larger ships because there is more rank to be had on them, but no destroyerman would rather sail on anything else.

The destroyer X is a personal ship and a personality. She is worked quietly. No one ever raises his voice. The captain is soft-spoken and so is everyone else. Orders are given in the same low tone as requests for salt in the wardroom. The discipline is exact and punctilious but it seems to be almost mutually enforced, not from above. The captain will say, "So many men have shore leave. The first man who comes back drunk removes shore liberty for everyone." It is very simple. The crew would discipline anyone who jeopardized the liberty of the whole ship. So they come back in good shape and on time. The X has very few brig cases.

When the X is in a combat area she never relaxes. The men sleep in their clothes. The irritating blatting sound which means "action stations" is designed to break through sleep. It sounds like the braying of some metallic mule, and the reaction to it is instant. There is a scurrying of feet in the passageways and the clatter of feet on the ladders and in a few seconds the X is bristling with manned and waiting guns, AAs that peer at the sky and the five-inch guns which can fire at the sky too.

The crouched and helmeted men can get to their stations

in less than a minute. There is no hurry or fuss. They have done it hundreds of times. And then a soft-spoken word from the bridge into a telephone will turn the X into a fire-breathing dragon. She can throw tons of steel in a very short time.

One of the strangest things is to see her big guns when they go on automatic control. They are aimed and fired from the bridge. The turret and the guns have been heavy dead metal and suddenly they become alive. The turret whips around but it is the guns themselves that seem to live. They balance and quiver almost as though they were sniffing the air. They tremble like the antennae of an insect, listening or smelling the target. Suddenly they set and instantly there is a belch of sound and the shells float away. The tracers seem to float interminably before they hit. And before the shells have struck, the guns are trembling and reaching again. They are like rattlesnakes poising to strike, and they really do seem to be alive. It is a frightening thing to see.

*　　*

A RAGGED CREW

December 1, 1943—When the plans were being made to capture a German radar station on an Italian island in the Tyrrhenian Sea, forty American paratroopers were assigned to do the job, forty men and three officers. They came to the naval station from somewhere in Africa. They didn't say where. They came in the night sometime, and in the morning they were bedded down in a Nissen hut, a hard and ragged crew. Their uniforms were not the new and delightful affairs of the posters. The jackets, with all the pockets, and the coarse canvas trousers had been washed so often and dried in the hot sun that they had turned nearly white, and they were ragged at the edges.

The officers, two lieutenants and a captain, were dressed in no way different from their men, and they had been months without their insignia of rank. The captain had two strips of adhesive tape stuck on his shoulders, to show that he was a captain at all, and one of his lieutenants had one strip of adhesive, while the second lieutenant had sewed a piece of yellow cloth on his shoulders for his rank. They had been ten months in the desert, and there was no place to buy the pretty little bars to wear on their shoulders. They had not jumped from a plane since they had finished their training in the United States, but the rigid, hard training of their bodies had gone right on in the desert.

There had been no luxuries for these men, either. Sometimes the cigarettes ran out, and they just didn't have any. They had often lived on field rations for weeks at a time, and they had long forgotten what it was like to sleep in a bed, even a cot. They had all looked somewhat alike, and perhaps this is the characteristic look of the paratrooper. The eyes were very wide set, and mostly they were either gray or blue. The hair was cropped, almost shaved, giving their heads a curious egg look. Their ears seemed to stick straight out from their heads, perhaps because all their hair was cut off.

Their skins were burned almost black by the desert sun, which made their eyes and their teeth seem very light, and their lips were ragged and rough from months of the sun.

The strangest thing about them was their quietness and their almost shy good manners. Their voices were so soft that you could barely hear them, and they were extremely courteous. The officers gave their orders almost under their breaths, and there was none of the stiffness of ordinary military discipline. It was almost as though they all thought alike so that few orders were necessary at all. When something was to be done, the moving or loading of their own supplies, for instance, they worked like parts of a machine, and no one seemed to move quickly, but there was no waste movement and the work was done with incredible speed. They did not waste time saluting. A man saluted his officer only when he spoke to him or was spoken to.

These paratroopers had as little equipment as you can imagine. There were some rifles, some tommy guns, and the officers had the new carbines. In addition, each man had a knife and four hand grenades, painted yellow, but they had had their grenades so long that the yellow paint was just about worn off. The rifles had been polished and cleaned so long and so often that the black coating was worn off in places and the bright metal shone through. The little American flags they wore on their shoulders were pale from sunburn and from the washing of their clothes. There was no excess equipment of any kind. They had what they wore, and they could carry. And for some reason they gave the impression of great efficiency.

In the morning their officers came into the conference to be instructed in the nature of the action. They filed in shyly and took their places at the long, rough table. The naval men distributed maps and the action was described in detail, part of it on a large blackboard that was set up against a wall.

The island was Ventotene, and there was a radar station on it which searched the whole ocean north and south of Naples. The radar was German, but it was thought that there were very few Germans. There were two or three hundred carabinieri there, however, and it was not known whether they would fight or not. Also, there were a number of political prisoners on the island who were to be released, and the island was to be held by these same paratroopers until a body of troops could be put ashore.

The three officers regarded the blackboard with their wide-set eyes, and now and then they glanced quietly at one another. When the discussion was finished the naval captain said, "Do you understand? Are there any questions?"

The captain of paratroopers studied the board with the map of the island, and he asked softly, "Any artillery?"

"Yes, there are some coastal guns, but if they use them we'll get them with naval guns."

"Oh! Yes, I see. Well, I hope the Italians don't do anything bad. I mean I hope they don't shoot at us." His voice was very shy.

A naval officer said jokingly, "Don't your men want to fight?"

"It isn't that," the captain said. "We've been a long time in the desert. My men are pretty trigger happy. They might be very rough if anybody shoots at them."

The meeting broke up and the Navy invited the paratroopers to lunch in the Navy mess.

"If you'll excuse us," the captain said, "I think we'll get back to the men. They'll want to know what we're going to do. I'll just take this map along and explain it to them." He paused apologetically and added, "You see, they'll want to know." The three officers got up from the table and went out. Their men were in the Nissen hut. The ragged captain and his lieutenants walked across the street, blinding in the white sunlight, and they went inside the Nissen hut and closed the door. They stayed a long time in there, explaining the action to the forty men.

*   *

VENTOTENE

December 3, 1943—The units of the naval task force made their rendezvous at sea and at dusk and made up their formation and set off at calculated speed to be at the island of Ventotene at moonset. Their mission was to capture the island and to take the German radar which was there. The moon was very large and it was not desirable that the people on the island should know what force was coming against them, consequently the attack was not to be attempted until the darkness came. The force spread out in its traveling formation and moved slowly over the calm sea.

On a destroyer of the force, the paratroopers who were to

make the assault sat on the deck and watched the moon. They seemed a little uneasy. After being trained to drop in from the sky their first action was to be a seagoing one. Perhaps their sense of fitness was outraged.

All along the Italian coast the air force was raiding. The naval force could see the flares parachuting down and the burst of explosives and the lines of tracers off to the right. But the coast was kept too busy for anyone to bother with the little naval force heading northward.

The timing was exact. The moon turned very red before it set, and just as it set the high hump of the island showed against its face. And the moment it had set the darkness was thick so that you could not see the man standing at your shoulder. There were no lights on the island at all. This island had been blacked out for three years. When the naval force had taken its positions a small boat equipped with a loudspeaker crept in toward the beach. From five hundred yards off shore it beamed its loudspeaker on the darkened town and a terrible voice called its proclamation.

"Italians," it said, "you must now surrender. We have come in force. Your German ally has deserted you. You have fifteen minutes to surrender. Display three white lights for surrender. At the end of fifteen minutes we will open fire. This will be repeated once more." The announcement was made once more—". . . three white lights for surrender." And then the night was silent.

On the bridge of a destroyer the officers peered at the darkness in the direction of the island. At the ship's rails the men looked off into the darkness. The executive officer kept looking at his wrist watch and the night was so dark that the illuminated dial could be seen six feet away. Gun control had the firing data ready. The guns of the whole force were trained on the island. And the minutes went slowly. No one wanted to fire on the town, to turn the concentrated destruction of high explosive on the dark island. But the minutes dragged interminably on, ten—eleven—twelve. The green, glowing hands moved on the face of the wrist watch. The captain spoke a word into his phone, and there was a rustle and the door of the plotting room opened for a moment and then closed.

And then, as the minute hand crawled over fourteen minutes, three white rockets went up from the island. They flowed upward and curved lazily over and fell back. And then, not content, three more went up. The captain sighed with relief and spoke again into his phone. And the whole ship seemed to relax.

In the wardroom the commodore of the task force sat at the head of the table. He was dressed in khaki, his shirt open at the throat and his sleeves rolled up. He wore a helmet, and a tommy gun lay on the table in front of him. "I'll go in and take the surrender," he said, and he called the names of five men to go with him. "The paratroopers are to come in as soon as you can get them in the landing boat," he said to the executive officer. "Lower the whaleboat."

The deck was very dark. You had to feel your way along. The boat davits were swung out as they always are in action, and now a crew was lowering the whaleboat. They held it at deck level for the men to get in—a coxswain and an engineer were already in the boat. Five officers, armed with sub-machine guns clambered over the rail and settled themselves. Each man had a drum of bullets on his gun and each one wore a pouch which carried another drum. The boat lowered away, and just as it touched the water the engineer started the engine. The boat cast off and turned toward the shore. It was pretty much of a job of guess work because you could not see the shore. The commodore said, "We've got to get in and disarm them before they change their minds. Can't tell what they'll do if we give them time." And he said to his men, "Don't take any chances. Open fire if anyone shows the slightest sign of resisting."

The boat slipped toward the dark shore, her motors muffled and quiet.

*   *

December 6, 1943—There are times when the element of luck is so sharply involved in an action that sense of dread sets in afterward. And such was the invasion of the island of Ventotene by five men in a whaleboat. They knew that there was a German radar crew on the island, but they did not know that it numbered eighty-seven men, all heavily armed, and moreover heavily armed with machine guns. They did not know that this crew had ammunition and food stored to last six weeks. All the men in the whaleboat did know was that the Italians had put up three white flares in the night as a token of surrender.

The main harbor of Ventotene is a narrow inlet that ends

against a cliff like an amphitheater, and on this semicircular cliff the town stands high above the water. To the left of this inlet there is a pier and a little breakwater, unconnected with the land and designed to keep the swells from breaking on the pier, and finally to the left of the pier there is another inlet very like the true harbor, which, however, is no harbor at all.

The whaleboat with the five men in it approached the dark island and when it was close to the shore the commander shone a flashlight quickly and it showed a deep inlet. Naturally, he thought this was a harbor, and the little boat coasted easily into it. Then the light flashed on again and ranged about, only to discover that this was not the true harbor at all but the false inlet.

The whaleboat put about and headed out again and soon it came to what looked like a sand bar stuck out of the water. And again the light flashed out, and it was seen that it was a breakwater. Again the boat proceeded, but approximately ten minutes had been consumed in being slightly lost. The third try was successful and the little boat found the entrance of the true harbor and nosed into it. And just as the whaleboat put its head into the little harbor an explosion came from behind the breakwater, and there was the sound of running feet, and then from the top of the cliff there came another big explosion, and then progressively back on the hill more and more blasts.

There was nothing to do then but to go ahead. The whaleboat plunged into the pier and the five men leaped out. Behind the breakwater lay a German E-boat and beside her stood a German soldier. He had just thrown a potato-masher grenade at the E-boat to destroy and sink her. One of the American officers ran at him, and with one motion the German ripped out his Luger pistol and tossed it in the water and then put both of his hands over his head. The lancing light of a powerful flashlight circled him. The officer who had taken him rushed him to the whaleboat and put him under guard of the boat's engineer.

Now a crowd of Italians came swarming down from the hill, crying, "Surrender, surrender!" And as they came they dropped their rifles on the ground, in an unholy heap. The commodore pointed to a place on the quay. "Stack them there," he said. "Get everything you have and stack it right there."

Now the landing was crisscrossed with lights. The five Americans stood side by side with their guns ready, while the Italian carabinieri brought their guns and put them in a pile. Everyone seemed to be confused and glad and frightened. The people wanted to crowd close to see the Americans and at the same time the ugly pig snouts of the tommy guns warned them back. It is not reassuring to be one of five men who are ostensibly holding a line against two hundred and fifty men, even if those men seem to have surrendered.

Every one of the Italians was talking. No one was listening. And no one wanted to listen. And then breaking through their ranks came a remarkable figure, a tall gray-haired old man dressed in pink pajamas. He stalked through the chattering, shouting ranks of the carabinieri and he said, "I speak English." Immediately the shouting stopped and the ring of faces showed intensely in the flashlight beams. "I have been a political prisoner here for three years," the old man said. For some reason he did not seem funny in his pink pajamas. He had a great dignity, even enough to offset his costume.

The commodore asked, "What were those explosions?"

"The Germans," the old man said. "There are eighty-seven of them. They were set up with machine guns to fire on you when you entered the harbor, but when you landed troops in the false harbor and when you landed more troops on the breakwater they thought they might be surrounded, so they retreated. They are dynamiting as they go."

"When we landed troops?" the commodore began, and then he shut himself off. "Oh, yes. I see," he said. "Yes, when we landed troops." One of the officers shivered and grinned at the commodore.

"I wish those paratroopers would come in about now," he said.

"I wouldn't mind it either," the commodore replied. And he went on to the old man in the pajamas, "Where will the Germans go?"

"They'll go to their radar station to destroy it. Then they have some entrenchments on the hill. I think they will try to hold them there." And at that moment there came a very large explosion and a fire started back on the hill, a fire large enough so that it illuminated the little dock and the entrance to the bay. "That will be the radar station now," the old man said. "They are very thorough. Too bad the troops you landed didn't get there first."

"Yes," said the commodore, "isn't it?"

More Italians came down the hill then and deposited their arms. They seemed to be very glad to let them go. Apparently they had never loved their guns very much.

On the dock the five Americans stood uneasily and the safety catches were off their guns, and their eyes moved restlessly among the Italians. The firelight from the burning buildings high on the hill made deep shadows in back of the dock houses.

The commodore said softly, "I wish those paratroopers

would get here. If Jerry finds out there are only five of us, I wouldn't give any odds on us."

And then there was a sound of a boat's motor and the commodore smiled with relief. The forty-three paratroopers were coming in to the shore. "Give them a light, coxswain," the commander called. "Show them where to come."

*   *

December 8, 1943—The five men from the destroyer moved restlessly about the quay on the island of Ventotene which they had accidentally, and with five kinds of luck, captured. The paratroopers did not arrive. There was no sign from the destroyer standing off shore and minutes got to be hours. The dark town on the cliff became peopled with imaginary snipers and back on the hill where the Germans had retreated an occasional explosion roared as they blasted more installations. They didn't know how many Americans there were, and there were five, and the Americans did know how many Germans there were, and there were eighty-seven. This was very largely in favor of the Americans, because if the Germans had known— It is not a nice thing to dwell on.

Your impulse when you are alone and not knowing when

you are going to be fired on out of the dark is to keep moving, to pace restlessly about and to be very timid about getting a light of any kind behind you. This pacing about is probably the worst thing you can do. According to Bob Capa, who has been in more wars and closer to them than nearly anyone now living (and why he is living no one knows), the thing to do is not to move at all. If you sit perfectly still in the dark, he argues, no one knows you are there. It is only by moving about that you give away your position. He also holds that under fire the best thing is to sit still until you know where the fire is coming from. This is a hard thing to do but it must be correct, because Bob Capa is still alive. But every instinct is toward shuffling about and leaving the place where you are. But getting a light behind you is the worst. It seems to burn you in the back and in your mind's eye you can see what a beautiful target you are to someone out in the dark, you and that great black shadow in front of you.

There probably is nothing in the world so elastic as subjective time. There is no way of knowing how long it took for those forty-three paratroopers to get ashore. It may have been half an hour and it may have been three hours. It felt to the five men ashore like three days. Probably it was about forty-five minutes. The dark, hostile island and the dark water gave no comfort. But after an interminable time there was a secret little mutter of engines. Then out in the dark there was a little flutter of light. The boat was asking for directions. One of the officers on the quay got down on his stomach and leaned over the stone parapet and signaled back with his flashlight so that it could not be seen from the island. And at intervals he flashed his torch to guide the boat.

It came out of the dark abruptly: out of the pitch dark it

slipped noiselessly and bumped gently against the quay. And it was one of those boats even the name of which the Navy will cut out if I put it in, but the important thing was that there were forty-three paratroopers on board. They seemed to flow over the side; they were very quiet. Their captain went to work instantly. He sent out pickets before he had been one minute ashore, and they slipped away up the hill to guard the approaches to the harbor. Some crept up into the town, armed with their rifles and grenades, and they occupied the tops of buildings, and others went down to the beaches to watch the seaward approaches. Meanwhile a little gangplank was ashore, and the supplies were coming down onto the quay in the darkness.

In the middle of this work there was a growl of a plane overhead. The captain of paratroopers gave a curt order and the men took cover. The plane droned over, and as it got offshore again the destroyer burst into action. She flamed like a flowerpot at an old-fashioned Fourth of July fireworks exhibit. Her tracers spread like a fountain. And then she was dark again and the plane was gone.

The unloading continued until there was a pile of goods on the quay, rations in cases and boxes of ammunition and machine guns and the light sleeping rolls of the paratroopers. They did not bring any luxuries with them. They never do. Food and ammunition are their main interests. They get along with very little else. But on Ventotene they brought water too, in those handled containers which are used for both water and gasoline. For Ventotene has no water. In other times water barges came out from the mainland. The only local water is that caught in cisterns during the rainy months.

When the supplies were landed the three paratrooper officers and the naval officers gathered in a little stone building on the waterfront. And an electric lantern was on the floor and the doors and windows were shut so that no line of light could show out. The faces were lighted from below and they were strained faces, with the jaw muscles pulled tight. The maps were out again.

"I'm not going to throw my men against a bigger force in the dark," the captain of paratroopers said. "Jerry will be trenched by now. I'm not going to move until morning. We've only got half as many men and no artillery."

An officer said, "Maybe—maybe we could talk them out of it. Let's have some of the Italians in and see what we can do. The Jerry doesn't know how many men we have or how many ships. Let's think about that a little. It's just barely possible we could talk them out of it."

"How?" the captain asked.

"Well, would you let me go up with a white flag in the morning?"

"They'd bump you."

"Would you let me try?"

"Well—"

"Might save a lot of trouble—sir."

"We can't afford to lose officers."

"You won't lose me. Just give me a nod."

The captain looked at him for a long time and then he smiled thinly and his head dipped, almost imperceptibly.

                    *   *

      December 10, 1943—The lieutenant walked slowly up the hill toward the German positions. He carried his white flag over his head, and his white flag was a bath towel. As he walked he thought what a fool he was. He had really stuck his neck out. Last night when he had argued for the privilege of going up and trying to kid the Jerry into surrender he hadn't known it would be like this. He hadn't known how lonely and exposed he would be.

      Forty paratroopers against eighty-seven Jerrys, but Jerry didn't know that. The lieutenant also hoped Jerry wouldn't know his guts were turned to water. His feet sounded loud on the path. It was early in the morning and the sun was not up yet. He hoped they could see his white flag. Maybe it would be invisible in this light. He kept in the open as much as possible as he climbed the hill.

      He knew that the forty paratroopers were crawling and squirming behind him, keeping cover, getting into position so that if anything should go wrong they might attack and stand some chance of surprising the Jerry. He knew the fieldglasses of the captain would be on the German position, waiting for something to happen.

"If they shoot at you, flop and lie still," the captain had said. "We'll try to cover you and get you out."

The lieutenant knew that if he were hit and not killed he would hear the shot after he was hit, but if he were hit in the head he wouldn't hear or feel anything. He hoped, if it happened, it would happen that way. His feet seemed very heavy and clumsy. He looked down and saw the little stones on the path, and he wished he could get down on his knees to see what kind of stones they were. He had a positive hunger to get down out of line. His chest tingled almost as if he were preparing to receive the bullet. And his throat was as tight as it had been once when he tried to make a speech in college.

Step by step he drew nearer, and there was no sign from Jerry. The lieutenant wanted to look back to see whether any of the paratroopers were in sight, but he knew the Germans would have their fieldglasses on him, and they were close enough so that they could even see his expression.

It happened finally, quickly and naturally. He was passing a pile of rocks, when a deep voice shouted an order to him. There were three Germans, young-looking men, and they had their rifles trained on his stomach. He stopped and stared at them and they stared back. He wondered whether his eyes were as wide as theirs. They paused, and then a hoarse voice called from up ahead. The Jerries stood up and they glanced quickly down the hill before they came out to him. And then the four marched on. It seemed a little silly to the lieutenant, like little boys marching up an alley to attack Connor's woodshed. And his bath towel on a stick seemed silly, too. He thought, Well, anyway, if they bump me our boys will get these three. In his mind's eye he could see helmeted Americans watching the little procession through their rifle sights.

Ahead was a small white stone building, but Jerry was too smart to be in the building. A trench started behind the building and led down to a hole almost like a shell hole.

Three officers faced him in the hole. They were dressed in dusty blue and they wore the beautiful high caps of the Luftwaffe, with silver eagles and swastikas. They were electronics engineers, a ground service for the German Air Force. They faced him without speaking, and his throat was so tight that for a moment he could not begin. All he could think of was a green table; Jerry had three deuces showing and the lieutenant a pair of treys. He knew they had no more, but they didn't know what his hole card was. He only hoped they wouldn't know, because all he had was that pair of treys.

The Oberleutnant regarded him closely and said nothing.

"Do you speak English?" the lieutenant asked.

"Yes."

The lieutenant took a deep breath and spoke the piece he had memorized. "The colonel's compliments, sir. I am ordered to demand your surrender. At the end of twenty minutes the cruisers will move up and open fire unless ordered otherwise following your surrender." He noticed the Oberleutnant's eyes involuntarily move toward the sea. The lieutenant lapsed out of his formality, as he had planned. "What's the good?" he said. "We'll just kill you all. We've got six hundred men ashore and the cruisers are aching to take a shot at you.

What's the good of it? You'd kill some of us and we'd kill all of you. Why don't you just stack your arms and come in?"

The Oberleutnant stared into his eyes. He had seen the same look over the green table. That what's-in-the-hole look. The look balanced: call or toss in, call or toss in. The pause was centuries long, and then at last, "What treatment will we receive?" the Oberleutnant asked.

"Prisoners of war under Convention of The Hague." The lieutenant was trying desperately to show nothing in his face. There was another long pause. The German breathed in deeply and his breath whistled in his nose.

"It is no dishonor to surrender to superior forces," he said.

*   *

December 13, 1943—When the lieutenant went up to the Germans with his bath towel for a white flag, the captain of paratroopers, peering through a crack between two buildings, watched him go. The men hidden below saw the lieutenant challenged, and then they saw him led behind the white stone building. The watching men hardly breathed then. They were waiting for the crack of a rifle shot that would mean the plan for kidding the Germans into surrender had failed. The time went slowly. Actually, it was only about fifteen minutes. Then the lieutenant appeared again, and this time he was accompanied by three German officers.

The watchers saw him walk down to a clear place in the path and there pause and point to the ground. Then two of the officers retired behind the white building again. But in a moment they reappeared, and behind them came the German soldiers. They straggled down the path and, at the place that had been indicated, they piled their arms, their rifles and machine guns, and even their pistols. The captain, lying behind his stones, watched and counted. He tallied the whole eighty-seven men who were supposed to be there. He said to his lieutenant, "By God, he pulled it off!"

And now a little pageant developed. As the Germans marched down the path, American paratroopers materialized out of the ground beside them, until they were closely surrounded by an honor guard of about thirty men. The whole group swung down the path and into the little white town that stood so high above the harbor of Ventotene.

Since Ventotene had been for hundreds of years an Italian prison island, there was no lack of place to put the prisoners. The top floor of what we would call a city hall was a big roomy jail, with four or five big cells. The column marched up the steps of the city hall and on up to the third floor, and then the Germans were split into three groups and one group was put into each of three cells, while the fourth cell was reserved for the officers. Then guards with tommy guns were posted at the doors of the cells, and the conquest was over.

The lieutenant who had carried the white flag sat down on the steps of the city hall a little shakily. The captain sat down beside him. "Any trouble?" the captain asked.

"No. It was too easy. I don't believe it yet." He lighted a cigarette, and his shaking hand nearly put out the match.

"Wonderful job," the captain said. "But what are we going to do with them?"

"Won't the ships be back tonight?"

"I hope so, but suppose they don't get back. We can't let anybody get any sleep until we get rid of these babies."

A trooper lounged near. "Those Jerry officers are raising hell," he said. "They want to see the commanding officer, sir."

The captain stood up. "Better come with me," he told the lieutenant. "How many men did you tell them we had?"

"Six hundred," the lieutenant said, "and I forget how many cruisers offshore."

The captain laughed. "One time I heard about an officer who marched fifteen men around a house until they looked like an army. Maybe we better do that with our forty."

At the door of the officers' cell the captain took out his pistol and handed it to one of the guards. "Leave the door open and keep your eye on us all the time. If they make a suspicious move, shoot them!"

"Yes, sir," said the guard, and he unlocked and opened the heavy door.

The German officers were at the barred window, looking down on the deserted streets of the little town. They could see two lonely sentries in front of the building. The German Oberleutnant turned as the captain entered. "I demand to see the colonel," he said.

The captain swallowed. "Er—the colonel? Well, he is engaged."

For a long moment the German stared into the captain's

eyes. Finally he said, "You are the commanding officer, aren't you?"

"Yes, I am," the captain said.

"How many men have you?"

"We do not answer questions," the captain said stiffly.

The German's face was hard and disappointed. He said, "I don't think you have six hundred men. I think you have only a few more than thirty men."

The captain nodded solemnly. He said, "We've mined the building. If there is any trouble—any trouble at all—we'll blow the whole mess of you to hell." He turned to leave the cell. "You'll be taken aboard ship soon now," he said over his shoulder.

Going down the stairs, the lieutenant said, "Have you really mined the building?"

The captain grinned at him. "Have we really got six hundred men?" he asked. And then he said, "Lord, I hope the destroyer gets in tonight to take these babies out. None of us is going to get any sleep until then."

FOR THE BEST IN PAPERBACKS, LOOK FOR THE

In every corner of the world, on every subject under the sun, Penguin represents quality and variety—the very best in publishing today.

For complete information about books available from Penguin—including Pelicans, Puffins, Peregrines, and Penguin Classics—and how to order them, write to us at the appropriate address below. Please note that for copyright reasons the selection of books varies from country to country.

In the United Kingdom: For a complete list of books available from Penguin in the U.K., please write to *Dept E.P., Penguin Books Ltd, Harmondsworth, Middlesex, UB7 0DA.*

In the United States: For a complete list of books available from Penguin in the U.S., please write to *Consumer Sales, Penguin USA, P.O. Box 999— Dept. 17109, Bergenfield, New Jersey 07621-0120.* VISA and MasterCard holders call 1-800-253-6476 to order all Penguin titles.

In Canada: For a complete list of books available from Penguin in Canada, please write to *Penguin Books Canada Ltd, 10 Alcorn Avenue, Suite 300, Toronto, Ontario, Canada M4V 3B2.*

In Australia: For a complete list of books available from Penguin in Australia, please write to the *Marketing Department, Penguin Books Ltd, P.O. Box 257, Ringwood, Victoria 3134.*

In New Zealand: For a complete list of books available from Penguin in New Zealand, please write to the *Marketing Department, Penguin Books (NZ) Ltd, Private Bag, Takapuna, Auckland 9.*

In India: For a complete list of books available from Penguin, please write to *Penguin Overseas Ltd, 706 Eros Apartments, 56 Nehru Place, New Delhi, 110019.*

In Holland: For a complete list of books available from Penguin in Holland, please write to *Penguin Books Nederland B.V., Postbus 195, NL-1380AD Weesp, Netherlands.*

In Germany: For a complete list of books available from Penguin, please write to *Penguin Books Ltd, Friedrichstrasse 10-12, D-6000 Frankfurt Main 1, Federal Republic of Germany.*

In Spain: For a complete list of books available from Penguin in Spain, please write to *Longman, Penguin España, Calle San Nicolas 15, E-28013 Madrid, Spain.*

In Japan: For a complete list of books available from Penguin in Japan, please write to *Longman Penguin Japan Co Ltd, Yamaguchi Building, 2-12-9 Kanda Jimbocho, Chiyoda-Ku, Tokyo 101, Japan.*